Are You a Leader?

A Video Arts Guide

Video Arts is the world's leading producer and
distributor of training videos. There are now over
150 Video Arts titles in daily use by some 100,000
organisations worldwide spread throughout 60
countries. Between them they have won over 200
awards in major international festivals.

Video Arts programmes combine the highest
standards of production excellence with the
maximum training impact. The quality of the
research, writing, activity and production is
exceptional, and the 'So You Think You Can
Manage' series is designed to make available this
expertise, entertainment and long-established
success in handy book form.

Other Video Arts books
available in Mandarin

Are You Organised?
Working With People

Are You a Leader?

Video Arts

*Cartoons by Shaun Williams
and Alan Hurst*

Mandarin

This book is based on the following Video Arts training videos:

Where There's a Will . . .
Decisions, Decisions
Meetings, Bloody Meetings
More Bloody Meetings
Think Or Sink (The Video Think Or Sink was produced in
    association with Heineken. Programme Consultant Ben Heirs)
All Change – Change For The Better
All Change – The Shape Of Things To Come

A Mandarin Paperback
ARE YOU A LEADER?

First published in Great Britain 1994
by Mandarin Paperbacks
an imprint of Reed Consumer Books Ltd
Michelin House, 81 Fulham Road, London SW3 6RB
and Auckland, Melbourne, Singapore and Toronto

A CIP catalogue record for this title
is available from the British Library
ISBN 0 7493 1827 9

Printed and bound in Great Britain
by Cox & Wyman Ltd, Reading, Berks

Contents

1 Motivation –
Where there's a will . . .

The prospect of leadership is one which arouses a whole host of opposing emotions in different people. Some will approach it with trepidation, believing it to be a quality they were not born with and can therefore never hope to acquire. For them there is little satisfaction in being in charge of a team of people because they believe they are not able to make a good job of it.

The opposite reaction is that of the 'tin pot dictator'. This person is just as lacking in leadership ability but has no intention of allowing a little thing like that stand in the way. Instead, this manager believes that leadership simply requires a firm hand, good organisation and a determination to take no nonsense from truculent employees. Just as the reluctant ruler attempts to lead with timidity, so the dictator rules the roots with tyranny – neither of which is successful.

Fortunately for both of them the old conception that leaders are only born, not made, has been shown to be untrue. The Sandhurst joke of the commanding officer who says of one of his recruits, 'This young officer is not yet a born leader' shows just how ridiculous this idea is.

People have discovered that *leadership, like most skills, is something which can be learnt by anyone*. Which is not to say that an average departmental manager can be taught to lead an army of elephant-mounted troops across the Alps, or command an armada of ships to a great naval victory, but there is not much call for that particular brand of leadership in modern businesses.

The prospect of leadership is one
which arouses a host of opposing
emotions in different people

There are as many theories about what leadership should be as there have been leaders, so much so, that it sometimes seems as if every man or woman of influence has left behind them volumes of thought and pithy quotes on the subject. It may generally be agreed that leaders need to be strong personalities equipped with a clear sense of direction but beyond that there is a vast range of opinions and arguments. Below is just a small selection of some of the more memorable through the ages.

'If the blind lead the blind, both shall fall into the ditch.' Matthew xv, 14

'You can lead a horse to water, but you can't make it drink.' Origin uncertain

'If the trumpet give an uncertain sound, who shall prepare himself to battle?' 1 Corinthians xiv, 8

'People who are masters in their own house are never tyrants.' Napoleon I, *Maxims*.

'Education makes a people easy to lead, but difficult to drive; easy to govern but impossible to enslave.' Attributed to Lord Brougham.

'I see it said that leaders should keep their ears to the ground. All I can say is that the British nation will find it very hard to look up to the leaders who are detected in that somewhat ungainly posture.' Sir Winston Churchill in a speech in the House of Commons, September 1941

'The real leader has no need to lead – he is content to point the way.' Henry Miller, *The Wisdom of the Heart*, 1941

'A chief is a man who assumes responsibility. He says – "I was beaten". He does not say, "My men were beaten". Thus speaks a real man.' Antoine de Saint-Exupéry, *Flight to Arras*, 1942

'Men are of no importance, what counts is who commands.' Charles de Gaulle in *The New York Times* magazine, 12 May 1968

'If you don't drive your business you will be driven out of business.' B. C. Forbes, American publisher quoted in *Forbes* magazine, 1974

From benevolent to brutal, the quotes above show just how wide-ranging people's opinions of leadership are. What is certain, however, is that it can be learnt and should be learnt if managers want to show that they can get more out of people than would have been achieved had they not been there. If they have simply justified their position by establishing organisation – a system designed to get the work completed on time – they will have only been half a manager, and not a terribly good half at that.

Organisation only provides a framework for people to work within and is not a solution in itself. To get the best from a department the manager will need to balance organisation with an **awareness of the workforce** and their needs. For the truth is that real leadership lies in the **motivation** of people, an art which has gathered more than its fair share of mystique over the years.

Words like charismatic, inspiring and that old chestnut 'born leader', are too often scattered around anyone capable of marshalling more than passing interest from a group of people – a reverence which seems quite over the top when you consider that leadership skills are within the grasp of most of us. It is certainly true that everyone will use these skills in a different way, but the basic techniques are the same.

All a good leader needs is an understanding of how the techniques work in practice and, importantly, an awareness of the vagaries of human nature. As the old saying goes, 'There are no bad troops, only bad officers.'

Let's look at the story of Jobson, a manager in charge of the workforce at Lockstock and Barrell Dispatch Services. There is nothing wrong with his organisational skills – the whole operation ticks over with computer-like efficiency – but he has a staff motivation problem which threatens to lose the company a very important customer.

A delivery seems to have gone astray and to Jobson

this is just one more example of the shoddy standards of workmanship he has come to expect from his staff. They certainly look like a sorry bunch – apathetic, witless, and totally lacking in initiative – so Jobson is outraged when a computer comes to life to tell him the problem is of his own making.

From the computer he learns it is the leadership, not workforce, which is at fault. In his zeal to establish an ultra-efficient operating system he has forgotten one vital element – the human factor. The result, a dehumanised environment where staff couldn't care less. The computer goes on to explain how leadership depends on the motivation of staff, and sets out a plan of action for Jobson to follow.

Jobson rules the roost in his dispatch organisation, a place where de-motivation is practically endemic. Take Carlton, the fork-lift driver, for instance. He performs his tasks with all the imagination and enthusiasm of an automaton. His orders are to move boxes from A to B and this is what he does, mindlessly, even when pile B begins to get precariously high.

Moody, whose job it is to load pile B onto trailers, wanders in late again and listens indolently to a dressing-down from Jobson. The lecture over, he drifts off to his work station with the same unhurried pace.

Among the rest of an exceedingly motley crew we find people like Jack, a youngster who is more interested in playing with his broom and passing comments than he is in sweeping the warehouse; Melanie, who sees the office as a prison run by VDUs; and Roy, an Accounts Manager who lacks any semblance of drive or imagination.

Anyway, let's see how this particular manager learns from his own computer the art of changing from an organised manager into a leader. We find him in his pristine office, decorated with charts, plans, VDU screens. He is clearly Efficient. The phone rings. The caller is Mr Harris of Playtime Electronics.

> **Jobson:** General Manager.
> **Harris:** Ah – Jobson. Harris here. I'm phoning about our keyboards.
> **Jobson:** Oh yes, one second . . . Yes. They left here two days ago.
> **Harris:** Well if they did, I'd like to know why I've got my customers screaming for them!
> **Jobson:** What? Well, I can assure you, Mr Harris, that nothing could have gone wrong this end.
> **Harris:** Well, you'd better be right, because if you're not we won't be renewing our contract with you.
> **Jobson:** Well, I can certainly check, Mr Harris, but I think you'll find that . . .
> **Harris:** You check, Mr Jobson, and *you'd* better do the *finding*. Right.
> **Jobson:** Well . . .
> **Harris:** Right!

Jobson hangs up and starts thumping his computer keyboard.

> **Computer Voice:** How are you going to handle this one?
> **Jobson:** I tell you this. Heads will roll. Where the devil is that order?
> **Computer:** It's still waiting in Bay 7.
> **Jobson:** Oh no! What the hell is he doing . . . Did you . . . did you just *speak*?

Lips appear on VDU screen.

Computer: Yes, Mr Jobson.

Jobson: You know my name?

Computer: I know everything about this company . . .

Jobson: What's going on here?

Computer: . . . and its brilliant organisation. So I thought I ought to warn you that you're heading for a disaster.

Jobson: Nonsense!

Computer: You're about to lose one of your biggest contracts – with Playtime Electronics.

Jobson: Yes. Because some idiot's cocked up my entire system.

Computer: Want to know who to blame?

Jobson: I should say so.

Computer: You want me to spell it out?

Jobson: Yes, yes.

The letters J–O–B–S–O–N come up on the screen.

Jobson: *Jobson?* But that's my name!

Computer: And it's your fault.

Jobson: My fault? Have you seen my staff?

Computer: With good leadership this would never have happened.

Jobson: Leadership? Look, I am a manager and a good one.

Computer: Yes, you are. And you could become a skilful leader, too. But if you think you have nothing to learn about leadership, press EXIT.

Jobson: I will. Anyway, you can't learn leadership. You're either a born leader or you're not.

Computer: . . . a born leader or you're not. Yes, funny how a lot of people think that. But leadership is simply a combination of organising, which you're

13

good at, and motivating, which you're not.

Jobson: I am! I put a bomb under that lot at least once a day.

Computer: No, motivating people is freeing them to do willingly and well the job that has to be done and that's a technique which anyone can learn. Motivation is a simple matter of giving people confidence. Three kinds of confidence.

Jobson: What *do* you mean?

Computer: Press C for Confidence.

Jobson does so and reads from the screen:

Jobson: 'Confidence in the value of their job, confidence in their value as individuals and confidence in their value as a team.' Well, you've lost me now. I mean, how do you go about giving people – what do you say – (*Reads*) '**Confidence in the value of their job**'?

Computer: Ah. Press One.

Jobson does so and reads . . .

Jobson: 'Context, Example, Importance.' Very good. Clear as mud. Now if you don't mind, there's an awful lot I could be doing . . .

Computer: Let's look at the way you'll probably do it. First – **context**. I'll show you a few little films, just to make it easy.

The show starts. Jobson watches Carlton driving a fork-lift loaded with cardboard boxes. Jobson sees himself in action.

Jobson: No, no. Not there, Carlton. THERE. Use your head, man.

Carlton is confused. He looks at the load, tries to remember where it is supposed to go, gives up and reverses away. The Computer butts in.

Computer: Now Carlton, for instance, hasn't a clue why one box should go in front of the others.
Jobson: But so long as he does what he's told . . . oh!
Computer: A leader doesn't just tell people what to do. He carries them along with him. Why don't you try telling him precisely what he's doing?

The film again. Carlton is intercepted by Jobson as before.

Jobson: Oh Carlton – Carlton – that's a consignment of thermostats going to Foskett's Construction – special delivery.

Carlton: Why?

Jobson: Never you mind why, just . . . well, apparently there's a gang of heating engineers on the Dartford site waiting to install them.

Carlton: Dartford: Those dimmer switches are going to that site too. Shouldn't they go on the same run?

Jobson: Er . . . oh yes . . . why not?

Computer: You see? A spark of interest and initiative, because for the first time he understands the context of his job. Now what do you think of Melanie?

Jobson: Melanie? Well, she sets a fine example – doesn't care about the job, lazy madam.

Computer: But where did she get *her* example from? If you don't show an interest in her and her work, Melanie can't be expected to have much enthusiasm for it herself. But of course the opposite also applies.

A film clip. Jobson is on the phone.

Jobson: No problem, Frank. We can cope with a late collection. It will be our pleasure to sort it out. Good. Cheerio . . . Melanie! Frank said he was thinking of transferring some more of his business to us.

Melanie: Oh, nice to be popular! I'll get the late collection scheduled with deliveries right away to be on the safe side.

Computer: So, set an **example** of a positive approach to work.

Jobson: Yes, but look: it's the job that's important . . .

Computer: A good leader lets his or her people know how important their job is.

A clip of Jobson heading for his office. As he passes the door marked 'Accounts' Roy emerges mournfully.

Jobson: Where do you think you're off to? Haven't you number-crunchers got any work to do? And Roy – that list of last month's late-payers. On my desk. Three o'clock. Right?

Computer: Now, is that what you'd call a highly motivated Accounts Manager?
Jobson: Yes, all right. But do I have to go down on bended knee whenever I want anything done?
Computer: Perhaps not if Roy got some appreciative feedback on the **importance** of his department's work . . .

The film runs again.

Jobson: Er . . . Roy. Just thought that you'd like to know Head Office said your cost-analysis of the air-freight contract – absolutely spot on.
Roy: Every set of figures tells a story.
Jobson: Well, not to me they don't. How do you do it?
Roy: Professional secret!
Jobson: Oh! By the way, can I have the list of last month's late-payers?
Roy: On your desk at two.

Computer: So, whatever their position in your work force, make a point of reminding them every so often that you recognise the importance of the job they're doing.

Jobson: So you're saying: if you want to create an atmosphere in which people feel positively motivated towards their work, the first step is . . .

Computer: Give them confidence in the value of their job. Help them to understand the context of their job. Set an example of a positive approach to work. Feedback to people the value and importance of their function.

Jobson: Oh, I see. Just tell them they're all doing a splendid job and leave them to it. So much for organisation.

Computer: No, I didn't say you should lose sight of organisation. We are talking about adding a leader's other skills.

Jobson: Well, *this* leader has an important missing order to chase up. I think I have all the skills I can handle, thank you. I've enjoyed our little chat, but now if you'll excuse me . . .

Computer: Press Two.

Jobson does so, and peers at the screen to read the word 'Individual'.

> **Computer:** Yes. The leader's second technique for increasing people's motivation: give them **confidence in their value as individuals**, through Challenge, Praise, Concern.
> **Jobson:** Well, that's all we need – individualists.
> **Computer:** Not the same thing at all.

The film again. It shows Carlton unloading boxes. Jack creeps up and shoves the trolley on which Carlton is standing. Jobson sees this.

> **Jobson:** Jack! In here!
> **Jack:** Coming, Mr Jobson.

Jack follows Jobson into the office where he sees Melanie having trouble on her computer.

> **Jack:** Wotcha, Mel. Having trouble on the old Japanese piano, are we?
> **Melanie:** I can't find these old South-East order records.
> **Jobson:** Take these service sheets over to Maintenance, would you?
> **Melanie:** I'll do it Mr Jobson. I want a word over there anyway.
> **Jobson:** No Melanie – you've got your own job to attend to. The lad will do it.
> **Jack:** But it's miles.
> **Jobson:** GO! NOW!
> **Melanie:** Cheerio Jack. See you later.
> **Jack:** South-East order records, was it?

Jack leans over Melanie's shoulder and taps a few keys on her computer.

Melanie: Oh! You've done it!
Jobson: Will you GET OUT!

Computer: Challenge.
Jobson: Well, he is a challenge, that hooligan.
Computer: Do you know why someone like Jack becomes truculent? He happens to be a red-hot computer buff. Knows how to treat us. So it's no wonder he's bored stiff being labelled the office gofa.
Jobson: Well, that means I should offer him a challenge?
Computer: You should always encourage your people to realise their individual potential.

Another film clip.

Melanie: Oh, you've done it!
Jobson: Just a minute lad
Jack: I'm going, I'm going.
Jobson: So, what do you know about computers, then?
Jack: Enough.
Jobson: Could you find those records we seem to have lost?
Jack: Easy . . . There they are.
Jobson: Well, that's very impressive. Why didn't you tell me you could do this?
Jack: You didn't ask, did you?
Jobson: So Jack the Lad turns out to be Jack of All Trades. Well, well, well.
Jack: That's very good, Mr J.

Computer: Challenge your people. They will feel stimulated and involved if they feel their special skills are being used.

Jobson: All right – you're so clever – explain this. I've got a member of staff who is 'challenged' right up to the hilt. So why is she a pain in the ashtray?
Computer: Your Depot Administrator?

The film runs.

Erica: Mr Jobson . . . I really must protest.
Jobson: What is it now, Erica?
Erica: It's this youth you've been employing. I've tried to ignore him, turn the other cheek, but there comes a time when his insolence requires more than a sense of humour.
Jobson: Yes, yes, Erica. I'm sure he doesn't mean any harm. Look, I'm trying to track down a missing order . . .
Erica: Either he goes or I go.
Jobson: Erica, please. You know I can't just . . .
Erica: Very well, if you're determined to keep him on, I'm sure you can do without me.
Jobson: Don't be silly, Erica.
Erica: I resign.
Computer: You know what she's asking for, don't you?
Jobson: A kick up the . . .
Computer: Praise.
Jobson: Praise?
Computer: Yes. Appreciation, recognition, congratulations, thanks. If she deserves them.
Jobson: Well, of course she does. She's indispensible. I know that and she knows that.
Computer: But does she know that you know? Don't waste her enthusiasm. If she knew she was personally appreciated she wouldn't feel so compelled to draw attention to herself.

A film clip.

> **Erica:** Mr Jobson, I really must pro . . .
> **Jobson:** Ah, Erica . . . May I just say I was very
> impressed with the speed you got those cases of wine
> documented.
> **Erica:** Yes, that's all very well, Mr Jobson, but . . .
> **Jobson:** No, really. If there was a world docket-
> processing record, I think you'd be the holder.
> **Erica:** Oh – thank you very much Mr Jobson.
> **Jobson:** In fact I need your help right now, Erica –
> I'm going mad here trying to locate a missing order,
> and if anyone can do it . . .
> **Erica:** That shouldn't take long.

> **Computer:** Amazing what a long way a word of
> praise and appreciation will go. Now let's look at
> your problem with Moody.
> **Jobson:** Moody. My God!

More film. Jobson is in the depot turning over boxes. He
discovers those labelled 'Playtime Electronics'.

> **Jobson:** I don't believe this. Where the hell's
> Moody? . . . Where the hell have you been, Moody?
> Waste of time asking, isn't it? And it's nine thirty,
> Moody. Third time this week! Oh . . . Get your coat
> off and get stuck in. I am warning you, Moody, you
> are rapidly becoming a very serious cause for
> concern.

> **Computer:** Yes, **concern**. Showing concern is the
> third way a leader gives his people confidence that
> they matter as individuals. George Moody's got a
> problem you should be getting to the bottom of. And
> I don't call shouting at him 'showing concern'.

Jobson: Yes, but you've got to have discipline! I mean, you know I caught him napping on the job as well? All right. I mean, what should I have done?
Computer: Well, you could have asked him to come and see you in here. Then take a bit of time out to see if you can get to the bottom of his time-keeping problem. Treat him like a human being for a change.

A film is run.

Jobson: Sit down, George. Well, I think it's time we had a little talk. This is the third time this week . . .
Moody: So? What are you going to do about it?
Jobson: Look, George, your personal life is none of my business, but you being late and asleep half the time is. If you've got a problem, maybe there's something we can do to help.
Moody: The wife had an accident.
Jobson: Accident? I didn't know about this.
Moody: No reason why you should. She got her foot jammed in a bus door when it moved off.
Jobson: Is she in hospital?
Moody: No. She's at home now. But she doesn't sleep much, with the pain, and of course I'm doing the housework and shopping and so forth . . .
Jobson: Well, I had no idea, George.
Moody: No, of course not. I mean you can't go around asking everyone if their missus has fallen off the bus lately.
Jobson: I'm very sorry to hear all this, George. Well, look, if it's all right with you, I'll explain the situation to the others and see if someone can cover for you if you need to take a bit of time off.
Moody: Well, thank you, Mr Jobson. I appreciate that. And speaking of time off, I suppose I'd better get back to work.

Computer: If you show concern for your people, they will show concern for their work. And that's the second of the leader's three techniques for increasing people's motivation. Give them confidence in their value as individuals: Challenge and develop their potential . . . Praise them for work well done . . . Show concern for them as human beings.

Jobson: Well, this is all most illuminating. So the thing is to give them confidence in the value of their job, and in their value as an individual.

Computer: That's it.

Jobson: Didn't you say there was something else as well?

Help them to feel, think
and work like a team

Computer: Press Three. See? The third thing you have to do is **build them into a team**. Help them to *feel*, *think* and *work* like a team.
Jobson: Yes, but of course they know they're a team. They only have to look around.
Computer: And what do they see? A lot of different people doing different jobs.
Jobson: But they're all working to the same goal. I see to that. I keep the team together.
Computer: Do you?

Another film clip. Jobson is on the phone.

Jobson: Mr Harris! It's all in order. Nothing to worry about – just a slight hitch due to . . . well, you know as well as I do, the low quality of staff you have to get by on these days. Right. A.s.a.p. Right. 'Bye.

He hangs up and grabs the dispatcher's PA mike. .

Jobson: Will Miz Erica Langton kindly come to the General Manager's office at once and explain what the hell is taking her so long to sort out a very simple bit of organisation? Thank you!
Computer: Fault number one – running down the team. No wonder they don't always feel you're on their side. And fault number two: victimisation.

The clip continues. Roy emerges from his office.

Roy: Was that about Mr Harris's order? Only I think . . .
Jobson: Nothing to do with you. Get back to work.

Melanie looks up.

Melanie: Mr Jobson, here's the reorganised dispatch schedule.

Jobson: What? Oh, good. At least someone's using their head. Why can't you lot be a little bit more like our Melanie, eh?

Computer: Fault number three: leaving somebody out on a limb. And fault number four: favouritism.
Jobson: All right, all right. Point taken.
Computer: As leader, you should treat all the members of your team justly and equally; and it is very important to let them know that they can rely on you as the leader of the team for your support and your protection.

More film. Jobson on the phone to Mr Harris.

Jobson: Systems failure, Mr Haris. But we're sorting it out. Thank God we've got a good team here. 'Bye.
Melanie: We've got problems?
Jobson: Yes, Melanie, get everyone together for a meeting in ten minutes. OK?

Roy peeps out of Accounts, then sees Jobson and begins to retreat.

Jobson: You too, Roy. You're in on this contract.
Roy: Right.

Roy emerges. The others start to arrive. Erica, Moody, Jack. They look quite positive!

Jobson: Yes, I see – help them to **feel like a team**.
Computer: Very good. Now you've brought the team together, what's your next move?
Jobson: I suppose I tell them their orders.
Computer: Is that what you normally do?
Jobson: Oh, no, I've got a better system normally. Put it in writing. That way I can tell each of them

individually what I want.

Computer: But then they don't know what the others are up to, do they?

Jobson: They don't need to – and if ever they do, I put up a notice.

Computer: Does that offer any opportunity for discussion? Do you ever get any comeback?

Jobson: Well . . . not a lot.

Computer: Not a very effective way of communicating, is it? But if you brief everybody collectively, they'll begin to **think like a team**, they'll begin to think it's worth contributing their ideas . . .

The film is nearing its climax. The whole team are assembled. Jobson addresses them.

Jobson: Good, well we've got the Playtime order loading. But there's obviously something in the system which allows that sort of mishap to occur. So, I've called this meeting to tell you all . . . to . . . tell you all that I was wondering if any of you have any ideas?

Erica: Yes, Mr Jobson. I've always thought one of the problems is that our priority delivery bay is right up at the top end of the warehouse.

Carlton: Yes, it takes ages to get to it, when the stuff's all coming in from the bottom end.

Moody: Is there any reason why that bay shouldn't be in the middle?

Jack: That'd save time, because nobody would have so far to go.

Computer: Open a two-way channel of communication.

Jobson: Yes. Think like a team.

Computer: And then it's a simple step to helping them **work like a team**.
Jobson: But we already do that. Virtually . . . don't we?

The film hasn't finished. Melanie is looking flustered, Erica and Roy are in the corridor and Moody, Carlton and Jack are coming in from the warehouse through to the transport area (where drivers come in and out for their instructions) for a tea break.

Melanie: Carlton, has the Playtime Electronics stuff gone off?
Carlton: Just going, why?
Melanie: Can you stop it a moment?
Moody: Do us a favour, Mel. This is our tea break.
Jobson: What's going on?
Melanie: Mr Harris wants to be sure we can get the stuff down to Godstone by one.
Jobson: Harris! What does he want? Blood?
Melanie: George – would you have a look on the board and see what else is on the SE early run?
Moody: Not me, that's a Transport job.

Melanie's other phone goes.

Melanie: Jack, would you?
Jack: Why me? Erica's not doing anything.
Melanie: Oh, hell! Customer Services. Could you hold the line please? It's Mr Harris. What shall I say?
Jobson: If the system's working, it'll be there by twelve forty-five.
Moody: He'll never make it.
Jobson: He might. Tell him.
Melanie: It will be there by twelve forty-five, thank you. 'Bye.

Computer: Nobody lifting a finger to help poor Melanie. So much for team work.

Jobson: Yes, well my timetable does allow for tea breaks, you know.

Computer: Even so, it's your job as leader to get your team thinking 'My job is to help *us* to do *our* job'. To inspire the idea of helping each other out.

Back to the film. Melanie is on the phone as before. The others are milling about.

Melanie: I ask you. Godstone by one. What's the rush?

Jobson: Er. . . . any ideas what the problem is? Erica?

Erica: Because they've got restricted access hours in Godstone. After one you can't get a delivery vehicle to their door.

Jobson: Can he get it there on time?

Moody: Depends on how many other calls there are on that run. I'll find out.

Carlton: Shouldn't take more than an hour – on the motorway.

Roy: Southbound's closed, though. Lorry jack-knifed. Heard it on the radio.

Moody: He'll have to take that minor road, through Paxton.

Erica: You won't get far with a large truck. There's that low bridge at Paxton.

Carlton: A van will go under it all right.

Jobson: Good thinking. But can we transfer onto a van and get the stuff straight there?

Roy: If he hasn't gone. No, he's still there.

Jobson: Melanie, tell them we'll be there at twelve forty-five.

Moody: Definite!

Computer: Tell them *we'll* be there at twelve forty-five. I like the WE.

Jobson: Thank you.

Computer: When you work like a team, with everybody chipping in, between you, you get it right. And there you are: the third element in the leader's technique for motivating his workforce. Give them confidence in their value as a team. Help them feel like a team, think like a team, work like a team. And that's it. I promised you a simple set of techniques. Motivation in a nutshell. And motivation balanced with organisation equals leadership. And that equals efficiency, both in your daily routine and in dealing with a crisis. And speaking of a crisis . . . how are you going to handle your people in future?

Jobson: Give them confidence in the value of their jobs. By making the context of their job clear to them, setting a good example, and ensuring they know the importance of their job. Give them confidence in their value as individuals by giving them a challenge; and giving them praise so that they know their efforts are appreciated; and showing concern for them as people. Give them confidence in their value as a team. By helping them to feel like a team, think like a team and work like a team.

Now, can I go?

Computer: Yes. I'm sorry. I had to do it. If leadership were just a matter of organisation I could run this place myself. But you see I lack something you've got.

Jobson: What's that?

Computer: Humanity. The human element. And that's the other half of leadership. You need both.

Golden rules

1 Leadership is a skill and can be learned.
2 Motivation is freeing people to do willingly and well the job that has to be done.
3 A leader doesn't just tell; he or she carries people along.
4 Show an interest in the work of others and let them know it's important.
5 Challenge your people and encourage potential.
6 Show appreciation.
7 Don't run down your team; use praise when you can.
8 No favouritism.
9 Leaders get a team thinking 'My job is to help *us* to do *our* job'.

2 Decisions, decisions

Making decisions is one of the basic tasks of management, but it is also an area where a great deal of trouble often starts. This is not just because it may be a wrong one; there can be plenty of problems even with the correct ones. You, as a manager, may quite easily come to a decision in the privacy of your office. It is possible, however, that you are not the right person to be taking the decision at all. And if you are, have you given yourself every chance to ensure that it is the best one you can make – even that the decision to make a decision was right? And suppose you have – then what? You have to make sure that something happens. How do you set about that, and have you taken all practical steps to see that what happens is properly implemented – and that there are no unforeseeen snags along the way?

One obvious problem lies not in taking the decision itself but in communicating it to those who are affected. 'Why didn't they ask me?' or, 'I could have told them it wouldn't work', or even, 'We were not consulted, we refuse to co-operate with the decision' are common complaints. You may be thinking: 'But I don't take that kind of earth-shattering decision' – which is not the point. Virtually *all* decisions affect others, and if they are badly handled without sufficient forethought, follow-up, etc., the consequences can be considerable.

Of course, not all decisions are equally important, or of the same type. First, the emergency decisions which require clear, quick and precise action in a crisis. Second, the routine decisions of an everyday nature (approving a petty cash slip or agreeing to a minor change in a shift rota) – pretty simple, but never allow 'routine' to be a synonym for 'thoughtless'. Third, there are the debatable decisions, those which will involve changes and, needless to say, these are the decisions which demand the most time and the most preparation. Here are five vital stages which should be part of all such decisions:

1 Fact gathering
2 Consultation
3 Taking the decision
4 Communicating the decision
5 Following up

Do all managers follow these principles? Let's examine them in more detail, following the experiences of a particular manager, Alan Robinson, who was given the job of moving his company into a new office building. Everything has gone wrong. He is sitting in his office, alone and depressed, wondering what caused so many mistakes. Surely other people have had more difficult problems to cope with. How did *they* manage . . . ? Suddenly, as if in a dream, he finds himself before an examination board of four of history's great decision-takers: Field-Marshal Montgomery, Queen Elizabeth I, Winston Churchill and the man who organised the assassination of Caesar, Brutus. They take him, backwards in time, through the various stages of the office move and show him how he ignored or neglected all the basic principles of good decision-making. They also show him how their own great moments of decision would have worked out if Alan had been in their shoes . . .

Monty: What's the matter, man? Haven't you been

in front of a review panel before? Now, tonight, we're going to teach you a thing or two about how to take decisions.

Churchill: And how to get commitment to them.

Elizabeth: No good making a decision if thou canst not get it executed.

Brutus: Thus so.

Monty: Now, as I understand it, you're an ordinary, reasonably efficient young manager who got put in charge of the office move.

Alan: Yes, that's right.

Monty: Tell us about it.

Alan: Well, it began like this . . .

The scene shifts to that happy day when an exuberant Alan rushed in to show Mary, his secretary, the new plans.

Alan: Mary, the new offices are terrific! It's a smashing building. They'll be perfect.

Mary: Have you been there?

Alan: No, I've been with the architects. But I've got all the plans here.

Mary: You mean, you haven't actually seen it?

Alan: Oh yes, on Friday night. Only a quick look. I was a bit pushed. But it's all in the plans. Fine.

Mary: Lots of room?

Alan: Lots. Means we get the Design Department in too.

Mary: I didn't realise you'd got stuck with it. I thought you just had to make suggestions.

Alan: No. I've got to decide when we move, who goes where, which department goes first. The whole thing, I think. Yes, me and the Planning Manager. Well, you know, he understands these things. I mean, he is a planner. We're doing it together, but I'm doing most of it. See, I've worked out who goes in what part of the building.

Mary: Sales on the third floor?

Alan: Yes, next to the bar and restaurant, they'll like that. Accounts on the fourth with Design, Production on the fifth and PR on the sixth.

Mary: When are we moving?

Alan: Christmas. It's a pretty slack time for us.

Mary: But Alan, aren't Sales very busy then?

Alan: Oh yes, but moving doesn't affect Sales much, does it? They're hardly here. Nothing like the rest of us.

Mary: It must have taken you ages to work out the plans.

Alan: Yes, the whole weekend. I'll just ring the MD and tell him about it . . . Ah, hello sir. We've worked everything out. I've managed to get the Design Department in and I've given the architect the go-ahead on the floor. Er . . . yes . . . I'm sorry, sir. No, I'll call him straight away. I'm sorry.

Mary: What is it?

Alan: He doesn't want Design moved. He says the Board never . . . Oh, forget it. Hours of work that was.

Right from the beginning Alan had not distinguished himself. He *thought* he knew the scope of his responsibility, but failed to clear a fairly simple point with the Managing Director. There is obvious confusion about who is actually in charge of what, and some important preliminary work has not been done, ensuring that the work actually done has to be done again. Montgomery can spot a poor bit of staff-work and sums up very succinctly:

Monty: You hadn't **collected the facts**. You weren't crystal clear in your mind what decisions had to be made, and which ones you were in charge of. And then you didn't ask yourself what information you needed.
Alan: I did. I knew.
Monty: Did you ask Sales or Accounts or Production exactly what their requirements were?
Alan: I thought I knew.
Monty: And were you right?
Alan: Well, I did speak to the architect and the Planning Manager. I looked at the plans . . .
Monty: You can't tell everything from plans. You've got to get off your backside and go out and look for yourself. Do a reconnaissance. Imagine if you'd been running my battles!

Alan is forced to watch himself in Monty's place addressing his officers and generals . . .

Alan: Right, now here's what has been decided. At twenty-two hundred hours, the Fifth and Sixth Armoured Divisions will move through here, across the plain and make a big push here and here.
A general: Who's in charge of the operation, sir?
Alan: I am, I think, Me or Alexander. Or Patten. One of us. I'll find out.
General: About the terrain, sir, is it hard or soft?
Alan: The map doesn't say.
General: What has the weather been like?
Alan: Oh dreadful, hasn't it.
General: No, *there*, sir.
Alan: There? . . . Er . . . well . . .
General: Have the tank commanders got enough fuel, sir?

Alan: I expect so. They'd have said if they hadn't, wouldn't they?

General: Won't they need air support?

Alan: They'd better not. I spent the weekend working this one out.

General: It's Mr Churchill on the phone, sir. He wants to know why you're attacking the French.

Alan: Hello? Yes, I know they're our allies, sir, but that's exactly what'll give us the vital element of surprise . . . Stick to the Germans, right. But you did say 'big attack', you know. I mean, I put in a lot of hours on this plan.

Monty turns a withering eye to Alan.

Monty: See what I mean?

Alan: That's not fair. That's not what I was doing.

Monty: It's exactly what you were doing. You can't make proper decisions until you collect the facts. First, clarify which decisions are yours. Second, decide what information you need. Third, go out and get it.

Monty has given a crucial checklist. Of course, Alan will have to think hard about *how* to follow it. But good managers will certainly not make a decision without knowing what decisions are within their responsibility and they won't take them without knowing the facts on which to base that decision. They will also have mastered where to get those facts. For example, in many cases, somebody inside or even outside the company will have direct experience of similar decisions. *Never be afraid to draw on the experiences of others*. Nobody should want to overburden themselves with useless information, but once you know exactly what you are doing, and therefore what is relevant to your particular decision, *you cannot be too well informed*. So, once you are equipped, what then? Over to the Great Decision Makers:

> **Monty:** Now, once I knew what decisions were mine and what information I needed, and after I'd gone out and got it, then I could move on to the next stage.
>
> **Alan:** Giving orders?
>
> **Elizabeth:** No, thou nincompoop, CONSULTATION. Thou has heard of consultation?
>
> **Alan:** Yes, Your Highness. I just didn't think generals did much of it.
>
> **Elizabeth:** Of course they do, thou mooncalf. How else dost thou imagine a mere woman defeated the Spanish? By reading *Teach Thyself to Thrash Armadas*? Thou must **consult** those underlings affected by thy decision. Didst thou?
>
> **Alan:** A bit . . .

Once again a scene from Alan's past is flashed before him:

> **Alan:** Well now, I've called this meeting because as you know, I've been put in charge of the move and I wanted to consult all the section heads about it. Now I've drawn up these plans.

John Barton, Head of Accounts, bursts angrily into the room.

> **Barton:** What's going on?
>
> **Alan:** Ah, John, I wondered where you were.
>
> **Barton:** What's all this about my department moving?
>
> **Alan:** Well, I told you, didn't I?
>
> **Barton:** You did not.

Alan: I'm sorry, I thought I had, sorry. Look, sit down. Now's the chance for us all to discuss it.
Barton: When's it to be? Three weeks?
Alan: We're not actually discussing the timing of the move today, because that hasn't been worked out yet. But what we're discussing today is who goes where in the new building. OK? I'd like your views. This is what I've decided, sorry, worked out. The Sales Department will be a bit smaller because it's on the third floor, but that's, well, because the sales people are out a lot. Oh, incidentally, the bar and restaurant are on the third floor too, so that'll be nice, won't it? Now unfortunately there may have to be a bit of sharing of desks. Still, you've all got your own company cars, haven't you? So you can't complain. You know, swings and roundabouts. One drawback is that there isn't any room for your secretaries on the third floor, but we can move them up to the fifth floor, to the typing pool . . .

McDonald, the Sales Manager, has something to say . . .

McDonald: Who the hell do you think you are?
Alan: What?
McDonald: How dare you? We need company cars to do our work, so as to keep people like you in jobs. And what's all this about sharing desks? Are *you* going to be sharing a desk?
Alan: Er, no . . .
McDonald: Let's get one or two things perfectly clear before we go any further, shall we? My salesmen do not prop up bars, except when they have to go away on long boring trips on company business. They do *not* share desks and they *will* have their secretaries in their offices. All right?

Alan: They can't. There isn't any more room on the third floor.

McDonald: Then I'm not having the third floor.

Alan: You've got to. The Board has approved this plan.

McDonald: And how are you going to make me?

Deadlock. Lack of consultation has led to confrontation. Alan has broken every rule: McDonald may have a good case for not moving to the third floor, but Alan hasn't even troubled to find out. He may have a bad case, but Alan has not given him the chance to agree to move with a sensible discussion about the merits and demerits of the position. Moreover, by presenting his views so insensitively, he has made certain that the pros and cons don't come into it at all. By seeming to walk over the legitimate considerations of colleagues, he has walked instead into a hole of his own making. *Never spring a surprise you don't have to*. Even if you can't see a problem, others might. Queen Elizabeth who had to unite such diverse and eminent characters as Drake, Hawkins, Walsingham and Burghley at a supreme moment of crisis in national history, spells it out in words of more than one syllable:

Queen Elizabeth: Consider this well. Consultation is a process factual and a process psychological.

Alan: Come again.

Queen Elizabeth: Oh, stone the dagoes. Can't you manage anything over two syllables? All right, modern English. There's two dead good reasons for consulting people, baby. The first is to see if there are any facts you've missed or got wrong. You nearly always find there's something important you hadn't grasped. Right? That's the first reason. The second is

41

psychological. When you make your decision, some people may not like it, but you want them to carry it out with reasonable enthusiasm and without being obstructive about it. Well, before you decide, ask their opinion and *listen* to it! If people feel they've at least had the chance to influence your decision, they're going to feel much more involved and committed to it than if it is taken over their heads. I can imagine you in my shoes in 1588 . . .

Alan is in charge of the Armada.

Alan: Gentlemen, the Armada. I have decided we shall attack it in the Bay of Biscay.
Drake: Your Majesty!
Alan: Yes, Drake?
Drake: If we can assail them in the English Channel we can outmanoeuvre them and replenish our ships each day, Your Majesty.
Alan: Now, who's Queen around here?
Burghley: But surely you wish to hear your Council's advice, Your Majesty?
Alan: I spent the weekend on this, Burghley.
Walsingham: Yes, but Your Majesty . . .
Alan: Walsingham, are you disputing my decision?
Drake: Look, we *are* the sailors . . .
Alan: And I'm the bloody Queen. You'll do your job and I'll do mine. Now, go on, all of you, off to Biscay. What's the problem?
Hawkins: Er . . . I've got a migraine.
Drake: And I've got a bowls match.
Walsingham: My grandmother's dying.
Alan: You take a decision and they all get bloody-minded.

Consultation means 'to seek information or advice from and to take into consideration the feelings and interests of others'. Assuming that you are taking decisions that affect your team, it seems logical to consult them before deciding. *Before* is vital. This is not a process of asking for a blessing on a decision that has already been taken. You need to listen to what your team has to say. You cannot possibly be in possession of all the facts or have all of the ideas on what to do. The more brains the better. This is not consensus. You are not asking them to agree or take a majority vote on what should be done. This is a process of posing the problem and asking them how they suggest it could be resolved. It is unlikely that you will be **taking the decision** on the spot. Therefore, you can go away to think about the ideas and information they put forward. Above all, you will have given yourself the chance to consider your *options*. A precipitate decision, before you have gathered the facts, before you have properly consulted, and before you have weighed up the results of those consultations and any alternatives which may emerge, is rank bad management.

Remember also to consult those on the fringe of the decision. Managers often go to enormous pains to consult their direct staff but forget to consult employees who will be indirectly affected by a decision. For instance, if a new computer form for orders is required, in many cases the computer staff and the administration people will be consulted. But what about the poor salesman out in the field? He may well be the last to be told, long after the design decision has been taken, even though he is the one who is going to have to fill in the form.

Alan can see all this when it's pointed out, but he still has a problem:

Alan: I can see that the right decision is usually clear if you've prepared for it properly. But supposing it isn't. Supposing you've considered and consulted and gathered your options, and you still don't know what is right. What do you do then?

Monty: Toss a coin! If your decision is so marginal that you still can't decide, decide arbitrarily. But remember, if it comes down heads, be committed to heads.

Alan: Are you serious?

Monty: Serious and right. Once you've decided, you must give a commitment to your decision, otherwise you can't sell it to your chaps. Right, Prime Minister?

Churchill: I agree. And the next step is, **communicate your decision**. Make sure everyone knows what it is. Persuade them that it's right.

Alan: Persuade them?

Churchill: That never occurred to you, did it? You must be prepared to persuade others to follow your decision. Now, how did you actually tell them about your office move?

Alan: I just told them . . .

The scene shifts to moving day, and the results of Alan's idea of what constitutes telling . . .

Removal man: This is the Accounts Department, right?

Barton: Yes.

Removal man: Right. I'm moving you today.

Barton: Wrong. A week today. The Production Department moves today.

Removal man: No. That's a week today.

Barton: In that case, how do you account for the fact

that they are all packed up, sitting there waiting to go?

Removal man: I can't help that. My orders are to move you now.

Alan: What's the trouble?

Barton: This gentleman insists on moving us today, when we are not ready to move and Production are.

Alan: Well, why aren't you ready?

Communicate your decision to those affected

Barton: Because we're not supposed to be until next week.

Alan: Who told you that?

Barton: You did.

Alan: I didn't. I know precisely what I told you.

Barton: Well, apparently you don't. Anyway, he can't move us. Look at what he's brought – tea chests!
Removal man: What's wrong with tea chests?
Barton: You can't put all this expensive equipment into tea chests! We need specialists, someone who knows how to move computers, not wardrobes.

Churchill glares at Alan.

Churchill: So, that was your idea of a briefing, was it? Nobody knew what was said or to whom. Always brief in a group. You've got to give them the opportunity of asking questions. And you've got to make sure that everybody understands what you've said to everyone else. Imagine this in 1944. I can just see you in charge of D-Day . . .
WRAC: The Chief of Air Staff would like to see you immediately, sir.
Alan: I'm busy.
WRAC: He's heard a rumour from the Admiralty that D-Day is tomorrow.
Alan: A rumour? It *is* tomorrow!
WRAC: Does General Eisenhower know, sir?
Alan: Of course he knows. I had dinner with him on Monday. Don't the services ever get together? This is chaotic . . .

Churchill emphasises his point.

Churchill: When you have briefed people together, always back up your briefing in writing. People's memories are not perfect. So . . .
Alan: Communicate your decision.
Churchill: Exactly. Brief people together. Be prepared to sell your decision. Then, confirm it in writing.

Monty: Right-ho. After communicating your decision, what then?

Alan: Well, one hopes that it's acted upon.

Monty: Does one do more than *hope*? Does one check, for instance?

Alan: Of course. It's common sense.

Common sense, maybe. But giving an instruction and having it carried out are not the same thing. Inevitably, Alan overlooked this, so, as the staff arrive at the new offices . . .

Alan: What's going on?

McDonald: The chief fireman won't let us in.

Alan: Well, why won't he?

Fireman: Because the double fire doors have not been fitted on the landing.

Alan: I knew that. I gave *orders* to have it done!

Brutus, who knows a thing or two about **following up** an instruction, gives them the benefit of his experience:

Brutus: The order not only having been communicated, Alan, imperative it is that it is checked by with or from those people having to perform it.

Alan: Eh?

Brutus: All right. Once you give an order, you must check that it has been carried out. Suppose I had not checked *my* arrangements. Let's see how you would get on at the Forum . . .

Alan at the Forum.

Alan: Here comes great Caesar now. When I strike, strike with me. Hail Caesar!

Crowd: Hail Caesar!

Caesar: Hail myself! Ahhh . . .

Alan: Liberty, Freedom. Proclaim it in the market place. Caesar is dead.

But he has not checked. Caesar sits up.

Caesar: Hello, hello, I want to dial 999, I mean IX, IX, IX . . .

Brutus points accusingly at Alan:

Brutus: See? Check that your decisions are carried out correctly, and with commitment, so that you can put right anything that's going wrong.

. . . you sent a memo to Mr Owen asking him to change our sockets on the twenty-fourth of May . . .

Check that your decision has been carried out

Monty: Right. Let's have a quick re-cap, shall we? First, collect the facts. Clarify which decisions are yours, and then decide what information you need. Then, go out and get it. Then what?

Alan: Then, consult those affected and always identify who will be affected by your decision. Check the facts with them. Ask them for their opinion, and listen to it. Then take the decision. That means gathering all your options and deciding when you have to decide. And when that moment comes, be decisive. If you've got to toss a coin, so be it, but once you've taken a decision, be committed to it. Then, communicate your decision. Be prepared to sell it. Always brief in a group. And always confirm in writing. Then people will go along with your decision, providing that you've consulted them in the first place. And finally check that your decision has been carried out.

Monty: I think he's got it.

Queen Elizabeth: He hath it.

Monty: Jolly well done.

Churchill: Carry on!

Golden rules

1 Problems can arise with correct decisions as well as the incorrect.
2 Never allow 'routine' to become a synonym for 'thoughtless'.
3 Never take a decision you cannot implement.
4 The decision to take a decision is a decision.
5 Before making a decision, ensure it's yours to take.
6 Draw on the experience of others.
7 You cannot be too well informed.
8 Never spring a surprise you don't have to.
9 Consultation does not mean consensus.
10 Once it is taken, be committed to your decision.
11 Have the courage not to take a decision.
12 Decisions must be 'sold' to those affected.

3 Running a meeting

Are you like Tim? If so, you spend a lot of time in meetings, usually late for the next because the last one overran. You'll have to work late into the night because the day was full of meetings: you may only have the energy to keep going because of the odd snatch of sleep you manage at those meetings . . . Perhaps, like Tim, you actually chair some of those meetings, but perhaps you haven't often asked yourself whether they are all necessary in the first place or whether you are running them effectively. Certainly Tim hasn't. Let's judge him in action through several examples and give a verdict after each. All of us will recognise that the verdicts could apply equally to many of our own performances! First, here he is, late as usual, for a weekly production meeting. His colleagues are waiting impatiently . . .

Tim: Sorry I'm late . . . just been to the bloody planning meeting . . . went on and on as usual. Bloody waste of time. Well, nice to see you all again . . . er . . . now . . .

Ian: How long is it going to take this morning, Tim?

Tim: Depends what we've got to discuss, really.

Ian: Do you mind taking the things you need me for first? I should be on the floor . . .

Tim: I should think so. Well . . . nice to see you all again. Gosh, is it really a week since we met? Seems like yesterday.

Jack: It was yesterday.

Tim: What?

Jack: We had to make a decision on the overtime rates.

Tim: So we did! Oh well . . . Yes. Well, nice to see you all as I say.

David: What are we talking about this morning?

Tim: Yes, we'd better talk about that first. Ian's got to go pretty sharpish, so . . .

Ian: Tim, what have you got?

Tim: . . . Er . . .

David: I'd like to talk about the nightshift standbys.

Jack: That's OK, David, I had a word with Frank.

Tim: Well, what else have we got? I always think it's very useful to get together like this, you know, to see . . .

Ian: If there's any point in having got together.

Tim: What?

Ron: Oh Tim, I saw Hawkins on Friday.

Tim: What did he say?

Ron: He thinks we'll be fine until the last quarter. But he did point out that the new cooling system's got problems.

Tim: Well, I've been taking care of that. So, what else have we got to talk about?

Ian: Nothing for me.

Jack: No.

Ron: No.

David: No.

Howard: No.

Tim: Good. Right . . .

Verdict: A clear case of chairing a meeting without due thought and **preparation**. Nobody had anything they wanted to talk about; there was no agenda; the only topics raised were irrelevant to a *meeting*. They could have been dealt with on the telephone or in each other's offices. Yes, it was a regular weekly meeting but a moment's thought could have enabled Tim to realise that there was no point in having it *as such*. Never have a meeting just because, like Everest, 'it's there'. *Always cancel a meeting, even a regular one, if you can discover it will be a waste of everyone's time.* Ask yourself what would be the consequences of not having it. Remember that conducting a meeting means:

1 Preparing yourself so that you are quite clear what the meeting is for.
2 Making sure that everybody else is clear as well.

The Company may have closed down, gentlemen, but the first Wednesday of the month still comes round . . .

Never have a meeting just because it's there

The second example finds Tim slightly better prepared. At least he has an agenda . . .

Tim: Right. Everyone got the agenda? Item One. Improving company communications. I think we all understand the problem. Ron?

Ron: It's a problem all right. It'll cost a lot of money to solve it.

Jack: You mean staff costs?

Ron: No, not staff. Equipment.

Tim: Surely it's management time at the root of it?

Ron: No. Equipment. At least six more video display units.

Tim: What?

Ron: Well, if you want Sales and Accounts to have direct access to data, the . . .

Tim: Look, Ron, we may be able to deal with this later on if there's time, but can we take Item One now?

Ron: I am taking Item One. Improving company communications.

Jack: No, no, Ron, it's not the computer, it's the telephones. Look, every time we try to get through down there, they're engaged.

Tim: No it isn't.

Ron: What?

Tim: I'm talking about the staff briefing sessions. How we brief the staff on this year's company results.

Jack: The company results? I thought you wanted an automated switchboard. You know the hold-ups we've been having down there.

Tim: Look, I'm talking about company communications.

Ron: So am I.

> **Jack:** So am I. How can we communicate if the
> phone's always busy?
> **Tim:** Look, the whole point of this was to get ideas
> on how to brief staff on this year's company results.
> **Ian:** Well, why didn't you say so?
> **Tim:** I mean hasn't anyone done any thinking about
> this . . . ?

Verdict: Guilty of failure to signal intentions to the
meeting. An agenda is not just a list of headings to
remind the Chairman of the topics. It's a brief for all the
others to work from. It has to define the direction and
the area of the discussion and also its end purpose. Tim
had an agenda all right, but if an item means something
different to each person at the meeting it is worse than
useless. The Chairman not only loses control of the
meeting, but essential preparatory work will not have
been done. All members must be **briefed** so that the
agenda becomes common and instantly recognisable
ground.

So make it clear to everybody what is being discussed,
why it's being discussed, and what you hope to achieve
from the discussion. Anticipate the information you and
the others will need and make sure you all have it.

The third meeting sees Tim with a better-planned
agenda:

> **Tim:** Right, that's Item One. For decision, allocation
> of parking spaces in the New Park. Six spaces for
> Marketing and PR. Four each for Production,
> Management and Works Management. And eight for
> Admin.
> **Marcus:** For review after three months.
> **Tim:** Yes, yes . . . God! Did that really take fifty
> minutes? Right. Item Two. For decision, McKenna

order for 250 L3s for delivery by 31 October. Do we accept the order or is 31 October too tight?

Marcus: The L3s are practically obsolete.

Tim: Marcus, they're not obsolete.

Marcus: Well, we oughtn't to be selling them. The L5s are more durable, they're easier to . . .

Tim: I'm sorry, I want to take this order.

Marcus: I think we're making a mistake.

Tim: Look, I'm sorry. It's ten to . . .

Marcus: Well if we hadn't spent fifty minutes discussing the bloody parking . . .

Tim: That was urgent. The New Park opens on Monday. Ron, how can we do this McKenna job?

Ron: We'll have to do L3s on number 2 and 3 machines, tomorrow and Thursday.

Tim: Right OK. That's it then. Now Item Three. For information. Forward Maintenance Schedules for batch-work machines. Ian?

Ian: Nice to get a word in.

Tim: Do you want to chair this?

Ian: Not *now*. I just want to say I've got to rewire number 2 and 3 machines over the next three nights.

Tim: Oh Christ!

Ian: I warned you last week.

Tim: Won't it wait till the weekend?

Ian: If you don't mind the place going up in smoke.

Tim: What about McKenna's L3s then?

Ian: Your problem.

Tim: Well, why didn't you mention this when we were discussing it?

Ian: I've been trying to.

Tim: . . . What can we do, Ron?

Marcus: Not take the order.

Ron: We'll have to put number 4 on to the L3s.

That'll mean more overtime.

Tim: Right. That's the plan. Any problems about overtime, Bert?

Bert: I'm not sure my members will agree to overtime. You see, we're a bit worried about the bonus scheme.

Tim: Right, well . . . we'll talk about the bonus scheme first now then. Then, if we can get that sorted out, we'll deal with the overtime. Then we can go back to Item Two . . . and see . . .

Marcus: Whether to take the McKenna order or not.

Verdict: Negligent ordering of agenda and criminal misallocation of time. Of course parking spaces were urgent and should have been Item One, but not being *important*, they should have been polished off in five minutes. The Chairman could even have put 'five minutes' against it on the agenda. Far worse was Tim's attempt to decide to accept an order before establishing that the men and machines were available to do it.

Perhaps you'd like to kick off, Peter, while the others gird their loins . . .

Work up the pecking order

Always look for logical connections between different items and **arrange them in the necessary order**. And **allocate time** so that the important items, even if they are the least urgent, get the fullest discussion.

The next example shows Tim handling a difficult problem:

Tim: Right. Item Four. Discipline. I don't think there are too many problems but I've got to review the discipline agreements with Bert this week, so what does anyone think?

Marcus: Well, they're still nicking knives and forks from the canteen.

David: I thought that had stopped.

Marcus: Oh yes it stopped, yes, for about ten minutes.

David: Well you expect a bit of that. How much is it going on?

Marcus: Enough.

Ron: My problem is that people are still clocking on for each other.

Ian: What your lads need, Ron, is a bit of discipline.

David: It depends what you mean by discipline.

Marcus: I'll tell you what I mean by discipline. Nailing a few of them to the front gates – that's what I mean by . . .

David: Oh shut up, Marcus. What I'm getting at is there won't be much of your kind of discipline till we get the hygiene factors right.

Ron: Well, which ones are still wrong?

David: Look, are we talking about problems or solutions? Because if it's solutions, we should start with trying to shorten discipline procedures.

Tim: I think we've got to review the problems first.

Ron: OK. Well, here's one. How can we really

expect a supervisor to control a group of forty-five?

Marcus: I'll tell you the problem. We can't even control the bloody supervisors.

Ron: They're all right.

Ian: So are mine. Good lads. I scratch their backs and they scratch mine.

Ron: No, it's much more a question of giving them fewer people to supervise.

Marcus: I'll tell you what's the problem. They're bone bloody idle. We ought to sack a few. That'd wake them up.

David: And get another Jones case?

Ron: Amazing, wasn't it? He was absolutely useless.

David: But we couldn't prove it, could we?

Verdict: A total neglect of **structure** and **control**. Tim hasn't presided over a discussion at all. It was more like a group therapy session. Discussions have to be structured, from the chair. First, state the proposition; second, produce the evidence and by all means allow arguments about what the evidence proves; third, come to a conclusion, and only then is the meeting in a position to decide on the action which should be taken in the light of that conclusion. Evidence must come before the interpretation of evidence, and interpretation before a decision on action. It is vital to keep these stages separate and to prevent people riding pet hobby-horses or going over old ground without regard to the proper sequence.

Finally, let's see how Tim handles a meeting which depends on the accurate recording of information and decisions deriving from a previous meeting.

Tim: OK. Last item. Ian, can you bring us up to date on progress on the pay structure review?

Ian: Well, I haven't been able to take it any further

really. I can't till the joint negotiating committee meets and decides about regrading claims. When are they going to meet, David?

David: But George was going to arrange that, wasn't he? He wanted to be there to put his case.

Tim: Ian, I thought you were going to fix a meeting quickly as you needed to know.

Ian: But Ron usually does that.

David: Usually yes, but as George said he wanted to be in on it, we said we'd leave it to him.

Ron: That's what I thought. We left it to George.

Ian: But George isn't here. I thought it was you, Ron.

Ron: No. George.

Ian: Would you like to take a vote on it?

Howard: Surely we decided that Ian would co-ordinate with George and Ron?

Tim: We agreed to take the necessary action.

Jack: Which meant Ron would make sure the committee consulted George.

Ron: Not in this case. It was George's job.

Tim: Next item. Item Eleven. To discuss and decide exactly what we did discuss and decide at the last meeting.

Ron: Before we decide that . . .

Tim: Well?

Ron: . . . oughtn't George to be here?

Tim: But I thought everybody knew what had been decided . . .

Verdict: A clear case of failure to **summarise** and **record**. Always summarise all decisions at a meeting, clearly and concisely, and make certain everyone has a chance to raise a point they are in doubt about. Then record the decisions immediately with the name of the person or group of persons responsible for any action. Ironically, a forum which, at its best, is a vehicle for communication, can too easily become one which leads to the opposite.

Golden rules

1 Ask yourself if the meeting is necessary. What would be the consequences of not meeting?
2 If you discover it will be a waste of time, don't hesitate to cancel a meeting.
3 An agenda is not a crib card for the Chairman.
4 A meeting should be a meeting of ideas rather than people.
5 Arrange the agenda in a logical order.
6 The Chairman is the servant of a group, not its master.
7 Always confirm action points to be followed by members, and record them.

4 More bloody meetings

We've looked at the *structure* of meetings. But of course
controlling a meeting doesn't depend only on structure,
essential though that is. It also depends on how you, as
Chairman, handle the *behaviour* of the participants.

A meeting isn't a battleground, but it can be a jungle.
We're all capable of behaving differently on different
days, at different meetings, with different people – and
consequently, we may all need handling differently as
the occasion demands. The Chairman's task is to plot a
skilful route through the jungle, however beastly people
may behave, and get the most out of the participants.

A meeting is a process, and a successful meeting is a
building process, where the Chairman promotes collab-

oration and avoids damaging conflict, combining all the positive elements from all the contributions made by different participants, moving forward despite awkward moments to add together all the good bits from suggestions and ideas to reach a positive, useful outcome or decision.

It's not the Chairman's task to batter the participants into submission; into accepting either his or her own or anyone else's views. The aim should be to **secure commitment to a consensus**. It really doesn't matter whether the meeting is formal or informal, peer-group or mixed levels of responsibility.

Everyone attending has a part to play, otherwise they shouldn't be there. The Chairman has to make them **play to the best of their ability, and as a team**; to maximise each individual's involvement, and get the best return from the meeting.

If you fail to build the right decisions, which people understand and agree with, then you will find it much harder to get people to implement them later. If people leave a meeting committed, they will be prepared to cope with any difficulties which might arise. There's no point in reaching a decision which nobody feels happy about, or which leaves half the participants at the throats of the others.

You don't necessarily need meetings to make decisions. Many would argue that you can make better decisions *without* meetings. So it's worth observing that the goal of any meeting should be to reach an outcome which the participants working alone could not have achieved – otherwise why bother? It's rather like the orchestra, which as a combination of individual instruments and sounds produces a result which none of them could have achieved separately.

All those who attend a meeting, therefore, should participate. What matters most is not the quantity of their participation, but the quality; and the Chairman must orchestrate them.

Every participant makes contributions, offers suggestions, puts forward ideas – and where the group wins over the individual is that by taking all the positive points from all the different participants, the meeting can build a better decision.

The Chairman must ensure that positive trends outweigh the negative ones, and that even if ultimately rejected, all suggestions are at least given an airing. Otherwise, participants will stop making contributions, or become demolition rather than construction workers, and the meeting won't achieve anything more than individuals working alone could have done.

The Chairman must keep all
the participants working together

Every meeting will have a mix of personalities. You're unlikely to have a meeting of all talkative types, or all strong silent types. Furthermore, we all tend to vary our behaviour as participants according to any number of factors. We can be argumentative or submissive, helpful or obstructive, on-the-ball or half asleep. We may be distracted by personal problems, or determined to have the final say whatever happens because we want to score points. The permutations are endless.

The Chairman must keep all the participants, whatever their personality or present disposition, working together during the meeting. He shouldn't expect to alter anybody's personality, but he can and should attempt to influence their behaviour. And we can take a look at types of behaviour which recur with regularity and can hinder the progress of the meeting. The Chairman needs to be on his guard for each of these, but by observing the Three Laws, he should be able to counter their effects.

What are the Three Laws? Let's look at a typical Chairman, male or female, reflecting in a dream. He, or she, is under interrogation and naturally claims the performance was rather more than adequate . . .

> **Chairman:** Oh yes, pretty good. I planned the meeting, I circulated agendas, I took minutes . . .
> **Interrogator:** We're not concerned with the mechanical side of the meeting. Only the human side.
> **Chairman:** Well, they all had cups of coffee, and pencils.
> **Interrogator:** And that takes care of the human side of meetings, does it? Well close your eyes, moonshine, and *think* about what happened. I'll be watching . . .

The Chairman does as he is told. He has Doug the Data Processing Manager on his right, Marcus of Sales on his left. Also present are Winnie, Head of Accounts, Eddie, Dispatch Manager, and Brenda, the Stores Manager. The meeting starts . . .

Chairman: Good morning. Right! Well, you all know what this meeting is about. You've got agendas, you've read the computer report, I've sharpened my pencil. So . . . away we go. Difficulties with the new computer system. First of all we'll agree what the problems are – get them out on the table. Then we'll try to agree why they happened and finally we can get down to how to solve them. Doug, why don't you put us in the picture?

Marcus: Picture? More like a disaster movie.

Doug: The main problems seem to centre around access to the computer terminals, hardware, downtime and user errors.

Marcus: If you ask me, the main problem lies with him and his Data Processing Department.

Chairman: Yes, well we didn't ask you, Marcus. Carry on, Doug.

Doug: There are worries about printouts.

Marcus: There's also worries about nitwits.

Chairman: Marcus, will you please let Doug put us in the picture.

Marcus: For God's sake, let's face facts . . . it's a cock-up. You know why? Because we've got a bunch of incompetents in the Data Processing Department.

Doug: We've got a bunch of incompetents all right. But not in my department.

Chairman: Well, we've got a bunch of incompetents. At least we agree on that. Good!

Marcus: Not in my department.

Doug: Oh yes they are. Input errors, procedure errors – want a list? Got an hour or two to spare?

Chairman: We're all busy men, Marcus!

Brenda: And women!

Chairman: And women, er, Brenda. Good point.

Marcus: Oh, for Pete's sake . . . Can we have a proper discussion?

Chairman: Well, we could if you'd just shut up for a minute.

Marcus: Why should I shut up? I've had this system up to here. And this meeting.

Chairman: You shut up because I'm the Chairman and I've told you to shut up.

Marcus: Better still, I'll go and do some work – instead of wasting my time.

Chairman: Sit down! Don't be so bloody childish. Thank you. Doug?

Doug: No, no . . . Marcus has got something to say.

Marcus: I'm the one who was told to shut up. Remember?

Chairman: When I said shut up I didn't mean . . .

Marcus: Shut up?

Chairman: What did you say?

Marcus: Shut up.

Chairman: Don't you tell me to shut up!

Back in the interrogation room the Chairman comes to . . .

Interrogator: Handled it well, eh?

Chairman: Well, I stayed in charge.

Interrogator: Yes, but what you were in charge of was a non-meeting. Sign this confession.

Chairman: What does it say?

Interrogator: It says that you broke the first law of

meetings.

Chairman: But I don't know what the first law of meetings is.

Interrogator: Then you can scarcely be expected to have kept it, can you? The first law of meetings is *Unite the group*. Get them all on the same side. Whereas you, very brilliantly, did the opposite. You let a fight start. You even joined in.

Chairman: Well, Marcus was spoiling for a fight.

Interrogator: All the more reason for you not to take sides. Tell me something, is Marcus always like that?

Chairman: No, no.

Interrogator: Exactly. But this morning something was bothering him. What?

Chairman: Well, do you know, I was wondering what myself.

Interrogator: Then why didn't you ask him? Go on. Eyes closed. Think back . . .

The Chairman's mind returns to the meeting . . .

Doug: Well, the main problems seem to centre around access to the computer terminals, hardware, downtime and user errors.

Marcus: If you ask me the main problem lies with him and his Data Processing Department.

Chairman: What's the trouble, Marcus?

Marcus: What do you mean?

Chairman: Well, you sound a bit angry about something.

Marcus: I'm not angry. I'm happy. Delirious.

Chairman: Well, we still need to know what the trouble is.

Marcus: Well, nothing. Except that I've just been told by some little Data Processing clerk that I'm not

allowed to tell customers when goods will be in stock
any more.
Doug: But you have full access to stock level records.
Marcus: Yes, but not to projected delivery dates of
out-of-stock goods.
Doug: You never asked for that.
Marcus: Well, I assumed you'd provide . . .
Chairman: Hold it. Look, Doug, delivery dates for
out-of-stock goods are a real problem for Marcus.
We'll put it top of the list – OK? Anything else
bothering you?
Marcus: No, no. Nothing in particular.

And back in the interrogation room . . .

Interrogator: So, you see what happens when you get
rid of the aggression. Aggression is the enemy of the
unity of your group. So never let people bottle things
up, let them let off steam. And don't take sides.
Chairman: No, no, right. I promise.
Interrogator: Good. Right, what other techniques are
there to reduce the aggression in your group?
Chairman: Ah . . . um . . . help me . . .
Interrogator: Excellent. A cry for help. And who is
there to help?
Chairman: Ah . . . the other people at the meeting?
Interrogator: Well done. Bring in the non-
combatants.
Chairman: But surely you don't want everyone
giving their opinions at the same . . .
Interrogator: I don't mean opinions. Stick to nice
neutral facts. From the non-combatants. It works.
Think back . . .

And back to the meeting . . .

> **Doug:** . . . input errors, procedure errors – want a list? Got an hour or two to spare?
>
> **Marcus:** When have I got time to spare? . . .
>
> **Chairman:** Hold it a moment. No point in having a punch-up . . . Brenda, what are the computer difficulties in Stores?
>
> **Brenda:** The main one is people making two entries for one order – one on acceptance and one when the invoice is issued.
>
> **Doug:** Well, that bears out what I said. In my opinion . . .
>
> **Chairman:** No opinion yet, Doug, let's stick to facts. Anything else, Brenda? Accounts, Winnie?
>
> **Winnie:** Just not enough terminal access time. Either something's blown, or someone's monopolising the entire system.
>
> **Doug:** What about slow screen response time?
>
> **Winnie:** That too.
>
> **Marcus:** Yes, that's a good point . . .

The interrogation room again . . .

> **Interrogator:** See how the temperature drops when you bring in the others? Nice neutral facts. So the first law is: **Unite the group**. Chief danger – aggression. Techniques: Let off the steam; don't take sides; bring in the others; stick to facts. Get it?
>
> **Chairman:** Got it!
>
> **Interrogator:** Good. Sign here please.
>
> **Chairman:** What's this?
>
> **Interrogator:** That is your second confession.
>
> **Chairman:** Oh, I see, I broke the second law of meetings too, didn't I? Of course. What is the second

law of meetings? Look, why don't you refresh my memory.

And back to the meeting.

> **Chairman:** Well, we seem to have identified the problems, delivery date information, data entry errors, delays and bottlenecks at the terminals. Anything else? OK, well . . . let's move on to the causes.
> **Doug:** There's only one cause. Learning to operate this thing needs effort. People just won't make an effort any more.
> **Winnie:** They will! I found Debbie almost crying yesterday because she couldn't get at the Accounts file.
> **Eddie:** Debbie? With the green Metro?
> **Winnie:** That's her.
> **Eddie:** Yes, she parked in my space this morning.
> **Brenda:** Your space? Think yourself lucky to have one. I suppose . . .
> **Marcus:** Yes, what I want to know is why has Bill Royce got two parking spaces? You can't come to work in two cars.
> **Eddie:** I think he lives in one. I've seen him shaving in it.
> **Marcus:** What are we talking about Bill Royce for?
> **Chairman:** Right, yes . . . let's get back to the point.
> **Eddie:** What point? What was the point?
> **Chairman:** Good point. Got it here somewhere. Ah, here we are, yes, I've got a bollard at the end of my parking space. Have any of you got a bollard at the end of your space?

Predictably, it's back to the interrogation room.

Interrogator: So, you see? The second law of meetings is to keep everyone to the point. **Focus on the group**. Go back and have another try.

The Chairman obediently does so.

Eddie: Her with the green Metro? She parked in my space this morning.
Doug: If people parked in the places allocated . . .
Chairman: We're getting off the point. Any other suggestions for causes of the computer problems?
Winnie: Really the trouble is people are forgetting their procedures. The back-up staff especially. They're very rusty.
Brenda: Can't we do anything about the suppliers? I mean about the servicing?
Doug: I've been on to them, they say they're doing their best.
Brenda: No, no . . . I mean don't they . . .
Marcus: I think we should recruit some people with some brains for a change. Especially in Data Processing.

The Interrogator leaps into action.

Interrogator: Well? How do you explain yourself?
Chairman: What? I didn't say anything wrong. I brought them back to the point.
Interrogator: But Brenda had a good point.
Chairman: About the servicing? But . . . I didn't even know what she meant.
Interrogator: Exactly! Why didn't you ask her? If you don't understand, how can the others? You should have tested comprehension.
Chairman: Tested comprehension? What does that mean?

Interrogator: It means making sure you've understood the contribution. Re-phrasing it if necessary. Off you go . . .

The meeting resumes.

Brenda: Can't we do something about the suppliers? I mean about the servicing?

Doug: I've been on to them . . .

Chairman: Well, er . . . hang on, I don't understand what you mean, Brenda, I mean . . . complain to them that the servicing is too slow?

Brenda: No, I mean don't they have different rates or something? You know, if we pay more, they respond quicker?

Chairman: Do they?

Doug: Oh, I see what she means. There is a four-hour call-out, but it's expensive.

Chairman: So what you're saying is that a possible cause of our problem is that we went for the cheaper servicing tariff?

Doug: It's a fair point.

And in the interrogation room:

Interrogator: And a fair point that didn't come out this morning because you didn't test comprehension. So the second law is **focus the group**. The chief danger is getting off the point. Techniques for focusing the group are to make sure every contribution is a relevant one. Keep a hand on the wheel and bring wanderers back to the point. And *test comprehension* so you make sure you understand and therefore make sure everyone understands.

Chairman: Unite the group. Focus the group. Can I go now?

Bring the wanderers back to the point

Interrogator: Go? What about your third crime?
Chairman: I broke the third law of meetings.
Interrogator: How?
Chairman: Pretty badly, I should think.
Interrogator: We'd better go back to the scene of the crime.

We do so.

Chairman: Right, well now . . . how do we put our computer problems right?
Brenda: Can we do something about training?
Marcus: We've done the training. No point in teaching if people are too stupid to learn.
Winnie: If people knew when the computer was available it might help.
Doug: They can always ask.

Eddie: I was looking through one of the manuals the other day. I'm not surprised that people make mistakes.

Marcus: Look, why are we beating about the bush? We all know what's got to be done.

Chairman: Right. What?

Marcus: Sack the consultants!

Doug: Hold on a moment.

Marcus: Look, Doug, everything we've said comes back to them. They were hired to make the system work. It doesn't. So get rid of them.

Doug: It's not all their fault. Some of it's ours.

Marcus: Sack ourselves, you mean?

Brenda: I was wondering . . . Are there . . .

Doug: It will take ages for new consultants to learn the system. Cost a packet too.

Marcus: Better than going along as we are.

Eddie: Look, there is an alternative . . .

Chairman: What do you suggest, Doug?

Doug: Well, if we think the consultants are the trouble, better get them in.

Marcus: Too right, we should get them in. Read them the Riot Act. Tell them that if they don't get it right in six weeks, they're out on their ears. OK?

Doug: If you like.

Chairman: Right, right. Fine, fine. Good, well, you'll fix the meeting then, will you, Doug? Good. Fine, fine. Well that's decided then. What the problems are, why they happened, how to tackle them. Good. Must go. Busy, busy, busy. Same time next week.

In the interrogation room . . .

Chairman: Well, what's wrong with that? I mean, we

made a decision, didn't we? A very, very decisive decision.

Interrogator: Yes.

Chairman: Well, that means a good meeting, doesn't it?

Interrogator: If it was a good decision. Was it a good decision?

Chairman: Goodish.

Interrogator: It was a rotten decision.

Chairman: Rottenish – but it was the will of the meeting.

Interrogator: Everybody?

Chairman: Everybody . . . ish.

Interrogator: You were bounced. A clear case of solutionism. Just plumping for a quick and easy decision.

Chairman: But you've got to plump for a decision in the end.

Interrogator: Wrong! You *never* plump for a decision. What do you do?

Chairman: You . . . unplump.

Interrogator: You *build* a decision.

Chairman: Build. That's the word I was looking for.

Interrogator: All of you together.

Chairman: Yes, but, I mean . . . most of them had their say.

Interrogator: Doug and Marcus did.

Chairman: Well, nobody else had any ideas.

Interrogator: Brenda was trying to say something. So was Eddie. The best ideas aren't always shouted. But you still need them. So bring in everyone who's got a contribution to make. The third law of meetings is *mobilise the group*. Get the group working towards a decision. Make sure everyone who's got something to say gets to say it. Otherwise, why have a meeting?

Chairman: But if they won't speak up . . .

Interrogator: Well, they won't if you let others squash them. You've got to protect the weak and keep the strong under control. Back you go and *do* get this right.

The Chairman rejoins the meeting:

Brenda: Can we do something about training?

Marcus: Training? No, get the consultants in – tell them everything's wrong!

Brenda: No, I mean . . .

Marcus: Read them the Riot Act and if it's not right within six weeks, they're out on their ears.

Chairman: Hang on, Marcus. Brenda, what did you mean by training?

Brenda: Well, all the training was done by the consultants . . .

Eddie: And the manuals – fat lot of use they were . . .

Chairman: Hold on, go on, Brenda. I'll come to you, Eddie.

Brenda: I think if heads of departments held their own refresher courses, we could get people to focus on the department's problems rather than on how the computer system works.

Doug: Actually, that's not a bad idea.

Chairman: Good. Anything else, Brenda? Eddie?

Eddie: Well, those manuals. I mean . . .

Winnie: I think that's right. No one can understand them. If we're doing our own training, why not write our own manuals?

Marcus: Yes, but they'll be useless without screen illustrations.

Doug: Well, that's no problem.

Chairman: OK. Anything else on training? No? Well, what about the problem of everyone trying to get to the terminals at the same time?

Doug: People can always check.

Chairman: Yes, but obviously they don't.

Brenda: We always seem to want to update stocks when Accounts are doing their bank entries.

Winnie: We have to do them before the banks close.

Chairman: You mean it would be all right after, say, about five?

Winnie: As far as we're concerned, yes.

Marcus: We ought to have schedules so we'll know whose turn it is.

Chairman: Can we have a schedule, Doug?

Doug: Easy.

Chairman: Any other ideas? Let's check round. Eddie? What about you?

Eddie: Well, I was wondering . . . there's a sort of link here, isn't there?

Marcus: Yes, the bloody consultants!

Chairman: Oh, what sort of link?

Eddie: Well, when we were installing the system, we didn't know a lot about it, so well . . . we let the consultants take all the decisions. Now we know what we want much better. Look, why don't we take over the training, write the manuals and make out our own user schedule?

Marcus: And where does that get us?

Eddie: I don't know.

Brenda: What we could do is sort of take over on the things we can do better now that we understand them.

Winnie: And get rid of a lot we don't need, and

perhaps get some enhancements as well.

Eddie: That's right. Us in the driving seat, them supplying what we ask for. I mean up till now it's been us servicing them.

Chairman: Doug?

Doug: I think that's right. If we could get them in for a whole day review meeting with all of us.

Chairman: Do I take it we're all agreed?

Brenda: It's a great idea.

Marcus: I suppose so.

A final interrogation:

Interrogator: You see? Better than sacking the consultants.

Chairman: Well . . . yes, yes, much better, yes.

Interrogator: So the third law: **Mobilise the group**. The chief danger is squashing. Techniques? Protect the weak and keep the strong under control. And when the group is mobilised to build a decision *check round the group*, collect all possible contributions, *record suggestions* – don't lose them, and *build up ideas* – don't knock them down.

Chairman: Right. Can I go now?

Interrogator: Yes, but only if you repeat the laws you profess to have learned.

Chairman: Oh no! I mean Yes! First law, unite the group. Chief danger – aggression. Techniques: let off the steam. Don't take sides; and bring in the others. Stick to the facts. Second law, focus the group. Chief danger – getting off the point. Techniques: stay alert. Keep a hand on the wheel. Test comprehension. Paraphrase or check back. Third law, mobilise the group. Chief danger – squashing. Techniques: protect the weak and keep the strong under control.

Check round the group and collect all possible contributions. Record suggestions – don't lose them. Build up ideas – don't knock them down.

Interrogator: Good! Well done. Now tell me about the first mistake. The one you made before the meeting began.

Chairman: Oh, the chicken vindaloo last night?

Interrogator: Not the vindaloo – the seating plan!

Chairman: Seating?

Interrogator: Yes, look . . . Doug and Marcus in opposite corners, set up for a fight, and both set up for a fight with you. Brenda stuck behind them and Eddie and Winnie pushed to the background to give them the smallest chance of being noticed. And you cut off from them all by a great desk barrier.

Chairman: Well, what am I supposed to do?

Interrogator: To start with – get rid of that frightful set-up. Rearrange the seats so that everyone can see everyone else. Sit yourself in the middle, then you can have Winnie next to you so you can include her more easily, and Eddie next to her. Brenda opposite you – she's not likely to pick a quarrel. Marcus next to you on the other side. You could put a friendly hand on his arm if he starts getting stroppy, and Doug next to him. Put them on the same side.

Chairman: And that does the trick?

Interrogator: Well, it's not infallible, but it gives the meeting a lot more chance than your way. Meetings are about human beings *and* agendas. Got it?

Chairman: Got it.

Golden rules

1 A meeting is not a battleground.
2 All members have a part to play or they shouldn't be there.
3 Decisions require the commitment of members to be effective.
4 Don't be 'bounced' against your better judgement.
5 Decisions sometimes have to be *built*.
6 Ensure full participation by everyone.
7 Your agenda is only as good as your meeting and what you get from the participants.

5 Think or sink – 'Decision Thinking'

Most good ideas come from people working in groups – Pythagoras was an exception. And those groups work best when they are well led. Leading does not mean dominating; it does not mean winning; it does not mean forcing your opinions through. It is far more subtle, for it involves the leader and the group planning their course together, providing choices, looking at dangers, opportunities, risks and rewards. It's called Decision Thinking, and there are four rules. Do you know them? Brian Barter didn't, so he lost his job. Arthur Allsopp did, and took over. Let's meet them as outgoing Barter hands over the last of his files to incoming Allsopp . . .

Barter: Well, there you are. I suppose I'd better wish you luck.

Allsopp: I'd better wish you luck, too.

Barter: What – with me going to head office and everyone knowing you've replaced me? You must be joking. So, what are you going to do that I didn't do?

Allsopp: Make a profit, I hope.

Barter: How?

Allsopp: I don't know yet. Where did you go wrong?

Barter: Go wrong? We didn't go wrong. It was bad luck.

Allsopp: But . . . even with hindsight?

Barter: No, it was completely unforeseeable.

Allsopp: Really? Will you tell me about it?

Barter: Well, it started at the original er . . . product relaunch meeting. Our best-selling chocolate bar needed a boost . . .

Barter recalls the meeting held some months earlier. Members of the Product Development Committee sit round the table. Brian Barter, Chris Cook from Marketing, Diana Davison from Accounts and Eddie Edwards from Production.

Barter: All right. Item Three. Now the Board's decision to relaunch 'Majesty' which has been losing market share for the past year? Any ideas?

Eddie: I had a thought about . . . er . . . you know . . . er . . . flow wrappings.

Barter: But we don't have the facilities here. That means bringing in the Northern plant.

Eddie: Yes, but . . .

Barter: Look, the Board want *me* to do this one, right? Or rather us. I'm not going halves with Peter Maynard and his rabble.

Eddie: They've done some good work.

Barter: Now look, let's get this straight, Eddie. I'm the one the Board asked for a proposal and I'm the one who's going to put it up. All right? So forget about joint solutions. Now come on. I said any ideas?

Chris: What about a new recipe variant?

Barter: That's more like it. Yes, I like that.

Diana: Aren't there a lot on the market already?

Chris: Yes, but there's always room for more, especially when it's new and exciting.

Eddie: That's quite true. Now if you started from scratch . . .

Diana: Have you got a concept in mind?

Chris: No, but I could work something out for the

next meeting.

Barter: I'll tell you what it's got to be. Right up the young end of the demographic market. Let's go for the twelve- to eighteen-year-olds who'll eat this instead of a meal – a substantial but sophisticated bar – with lots of fruit, nuts and raisins.

Diana: Don't you think it would be a better idea if we tried to . . .

Barter: Ah! Diana's got a better idea.

Diana: I wondered if it might not be a better return on assets if we went for the top end of the market – you know, aim for smart young adults by making it more self-indulgent.

Barter: No, I'm not going up the snooty end of the market. My brands are popular, innovative and exciting. That's what I'm famous for in this company. That's why they asked me and not Peter Maynard . . . Right, anyone got any other ideas? No? Right, so a low- to mid-range fruit-and-nut bar it is. Chris, can you get a marketing proposal together for the next meeting?

Chris: Yes.

Barter: Oh, and we'll need a relaunch timetable.

Barter has finished his recollections. Allsopp has a question.

Allsopp: That was *it*?

Barter: Yes.

Allsopp: That was *all*?

Barter: Oh yes. I don't mess about. Brisk. Decisive. Make your mind up and stick to it. Secret of my success.

Allsopp: But it flopped.

Barter: Yes. That was bad luck.

Allsopp: May I say something?

Barter: It's your division now.

Allsopp: It's a bit critical.

Barter: Don't mind me.

Allsopp: Well, to put it in the nicest possible way, that was the most crass, inept, uneducated and amateur piece of team thinking I have ever encountered.

Barter: We're not amateurs. We're professionals.

Allsopp: Professional manufacturers. Amateur decision thinkers.

Barter: What?

Allsopp: Well, didn't you notice one major obstacle to good thinking.

Barter: No, I did not.

Allsopp: It's got a name, actually. Ego. Someone's ego kept getting in the way.

Barter: What?

Allsopp: Remember this?

Allsopp produces a pocket tape recorder which mysteriously reproduces extracts from the meeting . . .

Barter: . . . the Board want me to do this . . . I'm the one the Board asked for a proposal . . . I'm the one who's going to put it up . . . Ah! Diana's got a better idea . . . Innovative, that's what I'm famous for . . . that's why the Board asked me . . .

Allsopp switches off the tape.

Barter: How did you do that?

Allsopp: I have my methods.

Barter: Well, when I said all that I was . . . I was . . .

Allsopp: A self-obsessed egomaniac who completely

failed to understand even himself. But you broke the rules as well.

Barter: No, I did *not* . . . Which rules are you referring to precisely?

Allsopp: The rules of good **Team Decision Thinking**. Have you never heard of the Four Stages of Decision Thinking?

Barter: 'Course I have.

Allsopp: What are they?

Barter: Er . . . Stage One, the beginning . . . the middle . . . the second half of the middle and er . . . Stage Four. I . . . I think there's some American guru who says something different. Remind me.

Allsopp: In Stage One we have to **develop a good question**. A helpful, sharply focused question. Remember yours? It was the amazingly helpful 'Any ideas?'

Barter: Well, I wanted suggestions.

Allsopp: Then why not an aircraft carrier. Or an egg whisk? Those are ideas.

Barter: That's silly.

Allsopp: So you agree. Ask a silly question, you get a silly answer. In Stage One you have to help the team and involve them in creating a good question.

Barter: What are you talking about?

Allsopp: Imagine this. I'm sorry if it seems a bit conceited but I'm going to describe that meeting with me leading it . . .

He does so. Everyone is taking at once . . .

Chris: Well, what about a new recipe variant?

Diana: Well, I think we should be . . .

Eddie: It would be perfectly easy to . . .

Allsopp: Well hold on, hold on. Let's try and focus

the question a bit more. What *sort* of brand are we looking to relaunch?

Eddie: Well, presumably we still go for the moulded chocolate bar.

Diana: Yes, but for which market – young and trendy? Middle-aged and traditional?

Chris: Ideally people who want a treat – something special.

Allsopp: But principally up-market.

Diana: But what sort of cost?

Allsopp: Our market has a cut-off at our present price plus 30 per cent.

Chris: Unless we go for a different market.

Diana: A new recipe *and* a new market? We need to turn this round fast, you know.

Allsopp: Exactly. So we're looking for an up-market brand, selling in a growth area of the over-eighteens and that can be ready to launch in the short term. Anything else?

Eddie: We don't want the new ingredients to deteriorate quickly.

Allsopp: Good point. And we don't want it to have a shelf life of under six months.

Allsopp finishes his description and turns to Barter.

Allsopp: You see? Building a good rich question takes time. But it's time well spent. Like taking time over the foundations of a building. Well, what do you think?

Barter: . . . They were all happy with my idea too.

Allsopp: Happy?

Barter: Well, nobody said they were unhappy.

Allsopp: Because you leapt in with it and challenged them to contradict you. You need to know *their* thinking before they know *your* thinking.

Barter: Yes, yes. Well, I'm sure that's all very well, but it doesn't mean that a new recipe variant wasn't a good idea.

Allsopp: No. But it might not have been the *best* idea. And it certainly should never have been the only idea. I mean, given a good rich question, you might have gone on to all sorts of things. Possibly even a different product group, you know, like box chocolates, sugar line novelties that you could have then promoted through hotels or airlines.

Barter: Yes . . . yes possibly . . . possibly yes.

Allsopp: Better ideas?

Barter: Yes, yes possibly . . . possibly better ideas. With hindsight.

Allsopp: Yes, but a good question provokes foresight. So. Rule One: Develop a rich question.

Barter: A rich question. OK, got that.

Allsopp: Good. So how did you get on with Stage Two?

Barter: Stage Two?

Allsopp: Come on, tell me about the next meeting you had.

Barter does so, reluctantly. Chris is presenting his proposal.

Chris: . . . and it's not only healthy with its extra nuts – but it's also very substantial.

Barter: That's pretty good.

Diana: But can we sell the same bar as a health food and a square meal at the same time?

Chris: Well, why not?

Eddie: Are a lot of outlets selling this sort of thing?

Chris: Not at the moment. But they're planning to.

Barter: And you can do it within the budget?
Chris: Umm . . . just about.
Barter: Good.
Diana: Isn't the cost a bit high?
Barter: I always say, manufacture up to a standard, not down to a cost.
Diana: Even so, we did some market research within the target age group.
Barter: That sort of market research is a waste of time. It just tells you what you already know.
Diana: I just feel it's very vulnerable to competition.
Barter: Why are you always so downbeat? Brighten up a bit, will you? I've always said they can't compete with the best ideas, they can only copy them. And we've got the best ideas. So shall we get on with it?
Eddie: Why not?

Barter comes to a halt. He looks anxiously at Allsopp.

Allsopp: Ever heard of rigor mentis?
Barter: . . . rigor mortis?
Allsopp: No. Rigor mentis. Rigid mind. It's a close relation of rigor mortis, though. Listen.

He gets out his tape recorder again.

Barter: I always say, manufacture up to a standard . . . that sort of market research is a waste of time . . . I've always said, they can't compete with the best . . .

And switches it off.

Barter: Well, it's . . . all true.
Allsopp: Sometimes. But you weren't saying it because it was true. You were saying it because it

saved you from having to think about what Diana was saying. *And* you squashed her, which was unforgiveable.

Barter: Sometimes people have to be squashed.

Allsopp: No. Ideas may have to be rejected. But people's feelings have to be protected. Otherwise they may not come up with any more ideas for you. Presumably it's that decision which sank the division?

Barter: No, no, *no*. It was *bad luck*. You don't seem to understand. There was absolutely nothing wrong with the decision.

Allsopp: Except that it was crass, inept, uneducated and amateur.

Barter: Look . . . costs overran, OK. The TV viewing figures were down because of the Indian summer, right? There was a poor response to our advertising campaign. There wasn't much response to the special offer. And our competitors cut their prices, damn them. It was just bad luck.

Allsopp: But it was still an *amateur* decision.

Barter: Why?

Allsopp: Because you didn't give yourself any choices. Just one idea, yes or no.

Barter: Well, what am I supposed to have done wrong now?

Allsopp: It goes back to the first meeting, actually. Remember your words? 'I'll tell you what it's got to be. Right up the young end of the demographic market. Anyone got any other ideas? So, a low- to mid-range fruit-and-nut bar it is. Chris, can you come up with a marketing proposal . . .'

Barter: So, what was wrong with that?

Allsopp: Why only one proposal?

Barter: Because only one proposal came up.

Allsopp: What bad luck . . . Look, this is Stage Two of Decision Thinking. **Give yourselves some options.** I'm sorry, but I'm going to take your place again.

Allsopp describes the scene with himself in the chair.

Diana: Have you got a concept in mind?

Chris: No, but I could work something out for the next meeting.

Allsopp: What sort of lines would you be working on?

Chris: Well, something fairly sophisticated.

Eddie: And expensive?

Chris: Yes. Because there will be a lot of fruit and extra nuts.

Allsopp: Good. Well, let's hold on to that. Right. So what else can we think of?

Diana: Well what about the other areas of the market, like the more traditional fifties and over?

Chris: The 'fifties and over'! Look here, we're going for the yuppies here, not the geriatrics. If you can't say anything useful, try a bit of silence.

Allsopp: Steady on, Chris. What . . . exactly did you mean, Diana?

Diana: Doesn't matter.

Allsopp: It does . . . go on.

Diana: Well, I thought . . .

Allsopp: Yes?

Diana: Well, you can still produce a high quality brand for that market which is just as sophisticated if you do it carefully – cut back on the razamatazz and keep it low key.

Allsopp: That's a very good point.

Eddie: Certainly if you left out the repackaging option, the costs would come down by as much as 15 per cent.

Allsopp: 15 per cent. So, Chris, your team will come up with costed proposals for a top of the range bar in quality packaging, a high quality bar with standard wrap, and a low-price small bar in the low-price wrapping.

Chris: Right.

Allsopp finishes and turns expectantly to Barter.

Allsopp: Good alternatives are the raw material of decisions. But all the team should contribute to all of them and they mustn't argue for just one each. So, given any alternatives would you still have chosen this kamikaze job?

Barter: Well, put like that and with the benefit of hindsight, and in the light of er . . .

Allsopp: In other words, you would not.

Barter: No, I wouldn't. Or rather, no we wouldn't.

Allsopp: And we didn't. Because we created some competition.

Barter: But when Chris got competitive you sat on him.

Allsopp: You need competition between ideas but co-operation between people. Competition between ideas is creative. Competition between people is destructive. So Stage Two is 'Help the team create alternatives'.

Barter: Let's see if I've got that. Stage One is create a rich question and Stage Two is create a choice of answers.

Allsopp: And Stage Three?

Barter: That's obvious.

Allsopp: Really? Well, how would you have handled it if you'd given yourselves some choices?
Barter: Like this. Do you mind using your imagination?

Barter embarks on his portrayal of the meeting which would have taken place . . .

Chris: . . . but all three are good concepts. It's a question of which way we want to go.
Barter: I must say I like this very sweet one. It's small, low-priced, definitely something that will appeal to the young teenagers.
Eddie: I can't say the top one grabbed me. The packaging is very dull.
Barter: What about the middle one?
Eddie: All much the same really.
Barter: Yes, I didn't like that so much. Too bland. Diana?
Diana: No, nor did I. No instant recall. I wasn't too happy about it. I didn't like the look of it, far too chunky. All a bit experimental.
Chris: But nothing completely untried.
Barter: Well, I'm with Diana.
Diana: I thought the top-range one was interesting. But then again, I'm not really sure.
Eddie: I didn't feel that was what the market wanted.
Chris: No, I rather agree, actually. I'm not too keen on that one.
Barter: So. It seems the low-price small bar gets the vote? Agreed . . . ? Good.

Barter looks at Allsopp, feeling rather pleased with himself.

Allsopp: Happy with that?

Barter: Of course. It's balanced, sensible. No messing about. And everyone got a chance to contribute.

Allsopp: Have you the faintest, slightest remotest idea of how professionals discuss alternatives?

Barter: Well, they . . . they look at each in turn.

Allsopp: And?

Barter: And . . . discuss them.

Allsopp: How?

Barter: They give their opinions.

Allsopp: No, they do not. No. They examine each one to see how *well* it might work out. Then they look at the dangers and create a 'worst case'. They don't just 'give their opinions'.

Barter: Well it depends what you mean by opinions, doesn't it?

Stage Three is a professional examination

Allsopp: For heaven's sake! 'I must say I like this very sweet one'; 'I can't say the top one grabbed me'; 'I didn't like the look of it'; 'I didn't feel that was what the market wanted'. Stage Three isn't a beauty contest – it's a **professional examination**.

Barter: Of what?

Allsopp: Of the future.

Barter: But you can't foretell the future.

Allsopp: No, you can't. But you can imagine it.

Barter: Imagine it?

Allsopp: Yes, you can ask yourselves a lot of 'what if . . .' questions. Look, do you mind if I take over again?

Allsopp does so and conjures up the scene:

Eddie: You're projecting a 20 per cent per year growth for this market sector?

Chris: Well, that's what the market analysts say.

Allsopp: Yes, but what if it's slower?

Chris: What if it's faster?

Diana: But according to the business plan the profitability is keyed to that growth rate.

Chris: That's true.

Allsopp: How many companies make this particular foil?

Chris: Well only one really, and they're in Germany.

Allsopp: If we have long lead times that might reduce our flexibility.

Chris: Well, they've been OK up until now.

Allsopp: Yes, but what *if* there are transport problems?

Chris: I agree. That would be serious.

Diana: How much scope is there for a price cut? If there's a price war, I mean.

Eddie: Which there could be.

Chris: Not a lot. Until you get into really high volume.

Diana: But if option three is only a small bar then I think . . .

Chris: Well, the small bars are very popular and the low price of packaging reduces the overall costs.

Allsopp: Eddie, any points on option three?

Eddie: No. They're all much the same really.

Allsopp: But what are the problems?

Eddie: I don't know. Not a lot.

Chris: Oh come on. Out with it, Eddie.

Allsopp: Eddie, there's something bothering you, isn't there?

Eddie: It's just that . . . you know . . . if we relaunch with the cheapest products, I mean our image is up-market. Not cheap and cheerful.

Allsopp: That's a very fair point. OK, so any snags with option two?

Diana: Well, if it's already a crowded area of the market . . .

The exchange between Allsopp and Barter is resumed.

Allsopp: Stage Three is where the pessimists and the nit-pickers come into their own. It doesn't always have the creative excitement of Stage Two. But it can save you millions. And you'll note that some people like to sit on the fence too much. Especially over the unwelcome but vital business of pointing out drawbacks and being the wet blanket. But they have to be made to commit themselves. So, was all that unimaginable?

Barter: No . . . all those problems could have been imagined.

Allsopp: Stage Three of professional decision making is trying to imagine the things that can go wrong as well as right. The team creates a good question, the team creates a choice of answers, and then we look at the dangers in each of them.

Barter: Look at the dangers. Well that'll just encourage the moaners.

Allsopp: Perhaps, but you look at the opportunities too. In any event, Stage Three must be done. And it takes vision and imagination to do it well. So, Stage Three: 'Assess the Dangers. But look at the opportunities too'.

Barter: Right. Well, that's it then really.

Allsopp: Really?

Barter: Well, we've been through the options. Now all we have to do is decide.

Allsopp: And how do you do that?

Barter: By becoming decisive. By . . . By going for it . . . No?

Allsopp: No. We start by reviewing the first three stages. This is where I take over again.

Allsopp depicts himself at the helm yet again.

Allsopp: So. We still think the three options are right. And we are asking the right question, Diana?

Diana: Except the point about sophistication and age groups.

Allsopp: Yes, an ideal brand would have potential appeal across the whole spectrum.

Eddie: We didn't think about the changes in legislation.

Chris: We didn't know about them.

Eddie: We do now, so we can take them into account.

Diana: And even in a recession we could still do well. People are more inclined to treat themselves to little luxuries when they can't afford the big ones.

Allsopp: Right. So let's look at the chances of success. Option one, Eddie?

Eddie: Well, it's more in keeping with our image. Best chance of success, I'd say.

Chris: There *are* more dangers to option two. So I'd stick with a 40 per cent chance for that and 70–80 per cent for option one.

Eddie: I agree.

Allsopp: Right. So . . . I've written these down . . . all of us feel that the probability of success with option one comes out at about 75 per cent which makes it a good candidate. Option two is 40 per cent and option three 50 per cent. Now, what about potential risk and potential gain?

Chris: Yes – we went through those. Option two could lose the most money, but the margin is bigger. It would be very profitable in high volumes.

Diana: But remember volume growth is more likely on the expensive brand, especially if it found a niche amongst young up-market adults. So its real profitability prospects are pretty low.

Allsopp: Actually I was impressed by the possibility of promoting it through duty-free shops.

Eddie: And it's less vulnerable to competition.

Chris: And a much higher margin in the outlets.

Diana: And it's good for our image.

Chris: We could promote it as a top quality bar.

Diana: 'The Executive Selection'.

Allsopp: That's very good. Very good, Diana. Right: So, option one: We have 75 per cent chance of success. Potential damage minimal. Potential profit is really quite good. Option two: We have 40 per cent chance of success. Potential damage serious. Potential profit not exciting. Option three: We have 60 per cent chance of success. Potential damage low. Potential profit respectable. So there you are. Which way do we go? Diana?

Diana: Well. I think it has to be option one.

Allsopp: Eddie?

Eddie: Option one for me too.

Allsopp: Chris?

Chris: I agree.

Allsopp: I go along with that. Option one it is.

Allsopp turns to Barter:

Allsopp: Got it? In Stage Four **the team review all the first three stages**. Circumstances may have changed. Your thinking may have progressed. And when you've reviewed the options, you have to look hard at the chances of success for each one, and then allocate a percentage value to each one. Finally, after the *chances* of success and failure, you look at the *consequences* of success and failure. And when you've looked at the potential cost of failure and the potential profit of success, you weigh the risks against the rewards. And that was Stage Four. Review the first three stages, and then decide on the chances of success for each option; and finally weigh the risks against the rewards. Now, do you think we made a good decision?

Barter: Well, as it happens, it would have made a lot of money. Still, couldn't be helped.

Allsopp: Well it could. With professional decision thinking from you and your team . . . So, back to head office?

Barter: I . . . I . . . don't really know yet. I mean I haven't made my mind up.

Allsopp: Well . . . why not decide professionally?

Barter: What? Oh – you mean . . .

Allsopp: Why not?

Barter: All right. Stage One: Develop a rich question, like: What occupation would be financially rewarding, professionally satisfying and personally enjoyable?

Allsopp: And open to a fifty-year-old executive who's just lost his company an awful lot of money.

Barter: Yes, yes, all right. Stage Two: Give yourself choices: back to head office, college lecturer, management consultant, or . . . unemployment benefit.

Allsopp: Or head in the gas oven.

Barter: No, no, we're all electric.

Allsopp: That's fortunate.

Barter: Stage Three: Er . . . assess the dangers. Back to head office?

Allsopp: Loss of face.

Barter: Lecturer?

Allsopp: Education spending cuts.

Barter: Consultant?

Allsopp: Credibility problem.

Barter: Unemployment?

Allsopp: Looks bad on job application forms. And Four?

Barter: Er . . . Four: Weigh the risks against the rewards. OK . . . Back to head office: chances 100 per cent; reward humiliation. Lecturer: chances 50 per cent; reward moderate. Consultant: chances 1 per cent; reward pretty good. And unemployment: chances 100 per cent; reward lowish.

Allsopp: So which is it to be?

Barter: I'm gonna go for number five.

Allsopp: Sorry. What was number five?

Barter: Electrocute myself.

Allsopp: No. I'd go for consultancy.

Barter: Chances 1 per cent?

Allsopp: No. Chances 100 per cent.

Barter: . . . sorry, I don't understand that one.

Allsopp: You see, I'm offering you a consultancy.

Barter: You want me to help with team decision thinking?

Allsopp: No. I want your help with brand development. That's what you know about.

Barter: Well, you wouldn't think it.

Allsopp: Well, nothing was wrong except the team decision making was amateur.

Barter: And you really think that I could learn Team Decision Thinking?

Allsopp: Yes.

Barter: Yes.

Allsopp: With a little help from your friends. Let's hear them.

Barter: You mean – Stage One: Develop a rich question. Stage Two: Give yourself choices. Stage Three: Assess the dangers but look at the opportunities too. Stage Four: Weigh the risks against the rewards.

Allsopp: Congratulations.

Golden rules

1 A big ego is a big enemy.
2 Creating a good question needs guidance.
3 Humiliating others is unforgiveable.
4 Give yourself alternatives.
5 Weigh alternatives by envisaging the future, what can go wrong as well as what may be right.
6 Look at the *chances* of success and failure and the *consequences* of success and failure.

6 How to change – change for the better

Maybe you've got a good company, successful routines and good profits. Why change anything? Well, first it's entirely possible that you could be even more successful with a few changes: somebody once said 'the good is the enemy of the better' which means exactly the same thing. But, more to the point, even if you are happy with the way things are, the world round you won't stand still. New technology, new fashions, market trends, population fluctuations, communication changes, government policies – there are any number of things happening outside which will sooner or later affect your business. Good leaders know this, so they don't manage it just for today but constantly try to manage tomorrow as well.

Manage tomorrow? Perhaps that sounds a bit like a shot in the dark, but it can be handled in a perfectly rational and professional way. To see how, let's join H. G. Wells, a man not only concerned with the future but able to pay it a visit in his celebrated Time Machine. He is on his way to the Kabul Olympics, 2028, but a machine breakdown brings about encounters with three managers peculiarly averse to change. Peter Mudd, Samantha Shortsight and David Groove. First port of call is Peter Mudd, startled when his unexpected visitor and grumbling Time Machine materialise . . .

Wells: Oh, forgive me, sir, the name's Wells. Herbert George Wells. And you are . . . ?

Mudd: The name's Mudd. Peter. But . . . where did you come from?

Wells: 1895.

Mudd: What? . . . How? . . .

Wells: How, sir? By means of this Time Machine. Stupid thing! Nothing but trouble ever since I modified the temporal drive.

Mudd: Well, you can't expect anything to work properly if you keep making changes.

Wells: And what do you have against change, sir? There wouldn't be a future without it, would there, or perhaps you disagree?

Mudd: I do. Take this Department. We've been issuing licences in the same way for years and years. Our well-known efficiency is based on hard work, good time-keeping and discipline. And that nothing changes.

Wells: Nothing changes? Not even the staff?

Mudd: Well, of course, people come and go . . . rather more often than I'd like, as a matter of fact, but otherwise . . .

Wells: Otherwise nothing changes – ever.

Mudd: Well, who knows what the future holds?

Wells: Well, I do actually, and by a strange coincidence I was passing through your future only the other day, and I have to say it didn't look too rosy?

Mudd: Why not?

Wells: See for yourself. I can play a bit of it back to you on this recording device here. If you go on the way that you're doing, sir, here's where your Department will be in about five years' time . . .

The recording device, actually a television screen, plays a scene from the future. A rather desperate Mudd is on the phone.

Mudd: Dregs Employment Agency? Mudd here, Nominal Licensing. Look, Personnel said you were sending over three applicants for the position of clerk this morning.

Dregs Employee: Haven't they turned up?

Mudd: No, they haven't.

Dregs Employee: Oh dear, not again.

Mudd: You know how desperate we are for staff.

Dregs Employee: You must be, otherwise you wouldn't have come to us.

Mudd: Quite. But I can't go on running this department single-handed.

Dregs Employee: It's not easy to find people with the qualifications you require.

Mudd: No, and when you do, you can't even get them to turn up for the interview.

Dregs Employee: I can't help that, Mr Mudd. Word must have got around.

Mudd: Word? What do you mean?

Dregs Employee: I'm sorry, Mr Mudd, but nobody wants to work for you.

Mudd: What? Listen, you sound a bright sort of girl. Just the type we need. It's interesting work, well paid, good prospects . . . I don't suppose you'd be interested in coming round . . . ?

Dregs Employee: Don't be silly, Mr Mudd. Good morning.

Wells switches off. Mudd is not surprisingly a worried man.

Mudd: Well, of course, it's always a problem getting and keeping staff. Oh God, we're not really going to end up like that in five years, are we?

Wells: I'm afraid so. Unless, of course, you change.

Mudd: Yes. But how can we be sure of making a change that's better than staying the way we are?

Wells: It's a skill. You can learn to choose the change that's right for you.

Mudd: Choose the change? How?

Wells: In three simple steps.

Mudd: All right.

Wells: And Step One is . . . '*Map your world*'.

Mudd: Brilliant! That is brilliant. What *do* you mean, 'Map your world'?

Wells: Well, to use your very own words: First, define your activity. Second, analyse its context.

Mudd: My very own words? When did I say that?

Wells: Oh, you haven't yet, but you will.

Mudd: And will I know what I'm talking about?

Wells: You tell me.

Mudd: All right. Define our activity. Simple. We issue licences – that's what we do.

Wells: And what about the way in which you do that?

Mudd: You mean the staff and I should all sit down and spend valuable time 'Defining our activity'? How we deal with the public, how we consult with each other, the hours we work . . . ?

Wells: Everything.

Mudd: And how, pray, will that tell us what needs to be changed?

Wells: On its own it won't.

Mudd: Ha! Not so clever after all . . .

Wells: . . . And that's why you must next analyse the context in which you operate.

Mudd: . . . Our context?

Wells: All the factors outside your control that affect the work which you do, from the cost of electricity, through the licensing regulations, right through to advances in computer technology . . .

Mudd: You can't analyse that lot – those things keep changing.

Wells: And you don't?

Mudd: Ah . . .

Wells: Why don't you?

Mudd: . . . Well . . . we don't actually need to. You see, we are a Local Department issuing licences. What we do is unique. We have no competitors.

Wells: I see. Not even for your workforce? What about the recruiting ad you put in tomorrow's paper?

Mudd: Yes, that should bring in quite a few applicants.

Wells: But will it bring in any staff?

The screen shows Christine Adams, an applicant for the advertised post of clerk, at her interview . . .

Mudd: Very good, Mrs Adams. You seem to be exactly the sort of person we're looking for.

Christine: Thank you.

Mudd: This is complex and demanding work, Mrs Adams. It calls for dedication, and of course punctuality. Staff are expected to sign in from 9.00 prompt to 5.30, no more, no less. Forty-five minutes for lunch. By permission . . .

Christine: Oh I see. Actually the children have to be picked up at 4.30, so I was wondering . . .

Mudd: Oh yes, I'm sure you can come to some arrangement for them. By permission . . .

Christine: Not really permission. It would have to be in the terms of employment. And as I will have the car here . . .

Mudd: Oh, you'll be driving in? Well, that'll take you another good hour in the rush hour.

Christine: That's why I thought if I came in half an hour early to miss the rush, I . . .

Mudd: Yes, but you won't find this door open till 8.59.

Christine: Well, I mustn't take up any more of your valuable time, Mr Mudd . . .

Mudd: You know, I haven't actually offered you the job, Mrs Adams.

Christine: No, but I do have one or two other interviews. Perhaps I'll get in touch later.

Mudd: Mrs Adams, you don't appear to be very keen to work for us. I can't understand why.

Back to the present.

Mudd: Yes, and I can understand *why* I can't understand why. It's not a bad job, good pay, regular hours, prospects . . .

Wells: But you've forgotten what I've told you. 'Mapping your world' doesn't just mean looking within these four walls. It's vital also to examine the context within which you operate. To look at the whole picture. Now, why don't you try again, picking up from where you left off. These things can be arranged, you know.

And so it is arranged . . .

Mudd: Mrs Adams, do you mean to say you are applying for other jobs?
Christine: Yes. Look, I've marked this newspaper. Quite frankly, some of these might be more suitable . . .
Mudd: What's the attraction with this one?
Christine: They have a staff car park. And a children's playgroup.
Mudd: What about this other one – you surely wouldn't rather work there? They're offering less money than we are.
Christine: They're also offering an extra week's annual leave, plus flexible working hours.
Mudd: I see.
Christine: And here I'm told they have wonderful new offices, and here at the school it would only involve working during term time, and here . . .
Mudd: Yes, yes, I get the picture. Mrs Adams, as I think you've gathered, I can certainly offer you a post here.
Christine: Well, to be honest, from what you've told me, I . . .
Mudd: Ah, but don't forget, we all have to move with the times, and, er . . .
Christine: You mean there are going to be some changes made?
Mudd: Yes, I think there probably are.

And in the present again.

> **Mudd:** Yes, I do see that once you make yourself look at the whole picture, you realise that you can't stand still. But you haven't shown me how to choose the change that's best for us.
> **Wells:** No, I haven't yet, but you've started right. You've drawn a picture of your situation – what you're doing, and what the world around you is doing.
> **Mudd:** But that's only the present – how do I look at the future?
> **Wells:** Ah, now, that's Step Two. And this is where the fun really starts . . .

But at that moment an alarm bell rings, lights flash on the machine and Wells jumps aboard.

> **Mudd:** Wait! What about Step Two?!
> **Wells:** I've got to go. Sorry. Look, I'll be back.
> **Mudd:** When?
> **Wells:** Later. Or sooner . . . But at least you've learned Step One. Map your world. Define your activity. Analyse its context.

Wells has gone. His next stop will not be Kabul, but the office of Samantha Shortsight, Merchandising Manager for Actiontogs Sport and Leisurewear. We join her as she is talking to her assistant, Janet, and showing her some impressive drawings . . .

> **Janet:** Hey, what's that?
> **Samantha:** It's a merchandising manager's dream. Attractive, stylish, reasonably priced . . .
> **Janet:** Now, that's exactly the look we've been trying to get. That's wonderful.
> **Samantha:** It's terrible. That is the opposition.

Fitwear.

Janet: What? How do Fitwear always manage to keep one jump ahead? This makes our stuff look really out of date.

Samantha: Not for long. You know me, the reflex kid. I want you to get on to Walter and hold up his series of press ads until I can get him some new drawings, then we'll have to get geared up for the shop displays.

Janet: But we've only just finalised the new season's range.

Samantha: Tough. Then come back and copy this memo to the branches.

Janet: OK. But they don't like all these changes.

Samantha: That's the name of the game.

Janet leaves, and as she does so there is a rumble, flickering lights and Wells and the Time Machine appear at Samantha's side.

Wells: Have I missed the pole vault?

Samantha: What?

Wells: Ah, this isn't Afghanistan, is it. Stupid thing! Er, would you mind terribly telling me the year?

Samantha: Who the hell are you?

Wells explains, recounting his experiences with Mr Mudd.

Samantha: But I don't understand what you say about selecting change. I think I've got a pretty good system.

Wells: Well, as far as you go, yes. You keep a very up-to-date Map of Your World.

Samantha: Yes, we regularly look at what we're doing and at what's going on in the world of leisurewear around us. That's what keeps us up with the opposition.

Wells: Yes, Mrs Shortsight, but 'keeping up' means never getting ahead, doesn't it – because you're not really looking ahead.

Samantha: In this business we're always looking ahead, to the next season.

Wells: Well, let's look ahead just a little bit further than that, shall we? This is Actiontogs in three years' time . . .

The screen is switched on showing Samantha's office with a rack full of sportswear and large quantities of boxes of Actiontogs clothing.

Samantha: This is our future, is it? That looks like a great new range. And look at all that stock ready to go out.

Wells: Listen a moment, will you?

He readjusts the volume as Janet comes into the office of the future . . .

Janet: They're not selling, are they?

Samantha: Of course they're not selling, otherwise the branches wouldn't be sending them all back here.

Janet: Well at least Fitwear made the same mistake.

Samantha: Oh, that could have been a golden opportunity for us.

Janet: Yes, if we hadn't been following their lead.

Samantha: Thank you, Janet. Anything else?

Janet: Yes. Another eighteen boxes downstairs.

Back in the present, Samantha stares at the screen aghast.

Samantha: Stop it! That is a nightmare. How could we have got it so wrong?

Wells: Because you're too busy making changes.

Samantha: But I thought that's what you wanted me to do?

Wells: No, no. You're constantly making emergency changes as a kind of knee-jerk reaction to what's happening to you. What you should be doing is carefully choosing the change that's going to benefit you most in the long run.

Samantha: I'd love to know how to do that.

Wells: Simple. Focus on the future.

Samantha: To see what's going to happen to us?

Wells: No, no, that's the common mistake. The skill lies in focusing on what's going to happen to the context in which you operate, and that's Step Two. That is: **Focus on the future.** Choose a point in the future. Research how your context will have changed. Pinpoint the needs and opportunities that will arise.

Samantha: Yes, but unlike you, I can't see into the future.

Wells: No, but you should be able to make some pretty fair predictions.

Samantha: Such as?

Wells: Such as that, thanks to my visit, your approach to change will be different by, say, tomorrow.

Samantha: Will it indeed!

Wells: Let me give you a sneak preview . . .

Wells presses buttons and suddenly it's tomorrow. Samantha is briefing Janet:

> **Samantha:** Oh, and Janet, could you just note that I want to talk about our future plans at the merchandise meeting tomorrow.
> **Janet:** The new winter range?
> **Samantha:** Yes, but I've been thinking we should look further ahead than that. We should be looking at where the future market will be, and who the bulk of our customers will be in, say, three years' time.
> **Janet:** But that far ahead you can't predict what everybody else will be doing.
> **Samantha:** The real trick would be for us to do what nobody else is doing.
> **Janet:** Yes . . . as long as it sells.
> **Samantha:** And it is the demands of the future market that ought to be our focus. I mean, should we be concentrating on sportswear for adults or children, or carry on catering for both?
> **Janet:** Well, the present sales figures show that we sell twice as many children's clothes as adults'.
> **Samantha:** But what about three years from now?
> **Janet:** You know, it's funny, Julian told me the South Street branch had three customers last week asking for long white flannels.
> **Samantha:** Really?
> **Janet:** Rather older than our average customer.
> **Samantha:** Maybe we should follow that up. In fact where was that article I was reading . . . about the changing age distribution of the population.
> **Janet:** Oh I saw that. The percentage of kids is falling while the percentage of the over-sixties is going up and up.
> **Samantha:** Chase up those figures for me, Janet.

We'll put it to the meeting tomorrow, and pick
everyone's brains about any other pointers they can
think of.
Janet: I could get on to the equipment manufacturers.
See if they're selling more of anything that might
appeal to the more mature end of the market. You
know, darts, croquet, bowls.
Samantha: Bowls?
Janet: Long white flannels . . .

The present again.

Samantha: All right. I can see that changes like age
distribution will affect our context.
Wells: Which is why you need to take Step Two.
Can you remember?
Samantha: Focus on the future. Choose a point in
the future. Research how your context will have
changed. Pinpoint the needs and opportunities that
will arise. Mind you, that can't be a once and for all
thing, can it? Maybe what we ought to do is to have
regular meetings to keep our focus on the future.
Wells: That's what I was coming to next. You
see . . .

But just then the Time Machine jerks, a bell rings and
Wells is on his way . . .

Wells: Sorry, the machine's starting up. I must fly or
I'll get left behind.
Samantha: What do I do next? What's Step Three?
Wells: Sorry – can't stop now. 'Byeeeeee . . .

And so to Groove's office. Wells is tinkering with his
machine, stranded again. Groove stands unhelpfully over
him.

117

Groove: Well, I can tell you that won't work.

Wells: Really.

Groove: And I'll tell you something else – neither will your fancy theories about 'learning the skill for choosing the best change'.

Wells: Oh dear.

Groove: No. You see, as a highly-regarded supermarket chain, we at Buyworld naturally keep a clear Focus on the Future. And what do we have to do to fit into the context we foresee? We have to get bigger.

Wells: Jolly good.

Groove: Rubbish. But because the rest of the Board think like you do, they've come up with this proposal which is going to change us completely. Never mind generations of experience, never mind the wishes of the customer – we've got to expand because it's the 'logical' thing to do.

Wells: Yes, but surely if it's the logical thing to do, Mr Groove . . .

Groove: That doesn't make it right. And, as Distribution Director, I told my colleagues what I thought about it, at yesterday's meeting.

Wells: Ah, well let's . . . let's just see how you put your case, shall we?

Wells presses a button and the screen shows Groove's office yesterday afternoon. Present are Groove, Alan from Accounts and Brian from Marketing. Groove is cross, brandishing the expansion proposal document.

Groove: You can forget it!

Alan: Ah come on, David. Centralised warehousing has to be the answer. Streamlined, bulk-based, economic . . .

Groove: Listen – from the very beginning Buyworld shops have been proud of their special character: supermarket efficiency with corner-shop quality and service. If we go over to centralised warehousing and bulk purchase, if we take the initiative away from the branch managers, what happens to that character? Supermarket efficiency, yes. But what else?
Alan: Supermarket profits.
Brian: We know this is the pattern for the future, Dave. Slikstore have already done it, and their sales are up by 15 per cent . . .
Groove: Oh surely we don't want to be like Slikstore!
Alan: Well we surely don't want to be like Counterwise – they've gone bust – didn't move with the times.
Groove: So, we're finished if we don't change? Well, believe me, we're finished if we do.

Satisfied he has made his point, Groove confronts Wells.

Groove: You see? It's a no-win situation. We'll end up with some half-cock compromise we don't really want, because nobody can find the right answer.
Wells: Oh no, you can always find the right answer . . . *if* you ask the right question.
Groove: What?
Wells: Good question. And the answer . . . Step Three. That is: **Design for the future**. Decide on the opportunities available. Shape your activities to fill them.
Groove: Yes, we've done that. And expansion, the 'logical' change, is destructive.
Wells: No, no. The right change for you doesn't mean destroying what you do best. The right change

means shaping and developing your activity to fill the new opportunities.

Groove: You mean . . . our proposals don't go far enough?

Wells: Perhaps that's something you should take up with your colleagues at tomorrow's meeting. Let's see you do it . . .

The button is pressed.

Alan: Quite simply, we have to change if we're going to stay in effective competition. And, if as David maintains, that means a reduction in standards, then regrettably that's something we have to . . .

Groove: Hold on, hold on. I've just remembered something somebody said to me . . . yesterday. I was going to say that the proposal will destroy our character because, with central ordering, it will be impossible to go on catering to our customers' wide range of tastes. But . . . are we right to assume it would be impossible?

Brian: Well, no, not impossible, but difficult – very difficult.

Groove: I'm thinking of a sort of specialist counter at each branch, catering for regional tastes, or local ethnic requirements. The sort of thing that our customers have come to expect and appreciate.

Brian: What, *ad hoc*, special orders, for a sort of gourmet corner?

Groove: Yes.

Brian: Costly – very costly.

Alan: Not necessarily. Not if we built extra flexibility into our delivery programme, but of course that would make the system awfully complicated.

Brian: But could we do it?

A quick return to the present.

Groove: Damn right we could do it. The system's going to be computerised anyway, so it could easily accommodate the complexities of ordering and delivery . . .

Wells: Yes, very good, but keep it for tomorrow's meeting, would you?

Groove: What? Oh yes, yes . . .

Wells: So my theory *was* right after all. The third step in choosing the change that's right for you is . . .

Groove: It's very simple. Design for the future. Decide on the opportunities available. Shape your activities to fill them. And there you have it. A neat handy formula for all. You know, everybody could learn how to have a positive approach to change if only they remembered those three simple steps. What did you say they were?

Wells: Oh, don't . . . don't ask me to go through them again, please . . . I'll tell you what . . . Fetch! Go on, fetch, fetch!

The machine vanishes, reappearing a moment later with a startled Peter Mudd and Samantha Shortsight on board.

Samantha: Where are we?

Wells: Well, Mr Groove here has kindly invited you to his office to tell him what you've learned. Mr Mudd, would you start?

Mudd: Well, I've learned that everybody has to be able to handle change, and it's vital to choose the change that's best for you.

Wells: And there's a methodical way of doing that which is?

Mudd: Oh yes! Step One, 'Map your world'. First, define your activity. Second, analyse its context. In my case, that meant seeing that we had to compete for our workforce, and would need to change our practices if we're to attract people to work in our Department. But what you didn't tell me is: what do I do next?

Samantha: Oh, I know that one. Step Two, you focus on the future. First, choose a point in the future and research how your context will have changed. Second, pinpoint the needs and opportunities that will arise. That gave me an exciting prospect of future growth. But how should we decide what to change in the way we operate?

Groove: I think I can help you there. Step Three. You design for the future. You decide on the opportunities available, and then you shape your activities to fill them. That doesn't mean you destroy your activity to fit the context. You develop it to fill the opportunities. In my case, that meant developing our operation to be effectively competitive while increasing the quality of service to our customers. And I don't need to ask you what to do next. Now we've all chosen a change for the better, we simply put it into practice. We can't go wrong.

Wells: Well, a lot of people do, you know.

Groove: I think you underestimate me, Mr Wells.

Wells: That would be impossible.

Groove: Thank you.

Samantha: Wait a minute – you mean we've still got more to learn?

But Wells is on board the machine, putting on his flying helmet and scarf.

Wells: Oh yes. But I'll come back and tell you all about it immediately after the Kabul Olympics. And now I must fly – otherwise I'll be late for the synchronised chicken juggling . . .

Golden rules

1 You may not want to change but the outside
  world will change anyway.
2 Emulating others means never getting ahead.
3 Choose the changes you make carefully,
  don't respond with knee-jerk reactions.
4 Plan your changes by focusing on the future.
5 Getting the right answer depends on finding
  the right question.

7 How to manage change – the shape of things to come

We left Mr Mudd, Mrs Shortsight and Mr Groove optimistic and confident. They took advantage of H. G. Wells' glimpses into the future, learned the lessons he taught them, and so set about putting them into practice. Now, just a few months later, they are glum, disconsolate and facing ruin. They are not pleased with their visitor from another time and are throwing moody darts at his portrait on the wall.

Samantha: I don't understand it. How did we all go so far wrong in just six months?

Groove: We listened to H. G. Wells, that's how.

Mudd: But the advice he gave us on how to change for the better made good sense. That's why we all followed it. And that way each of us was able to choose a change for the better.

Groove: So far so good. But when Buyworld Stores put that change into operation, well you wouldn't believe the resistance people put up.

Samantha: Don't tell me. Actiontogs were thrown into complete chaos.

Mudd: Well, the staff at the Licensing Department seemed happy about the change, but none of us realised how difficult it was going to be.

Samantha: To be fair to Mr Wells, he did say we had more to learn.

Groove: Then he should have stayed and helped us instead of swanning off to the Kabul Olympics for . . . for the synchronised chicken juggling.

And, right on cue, there is a rumble and a flicker, and H. G. Wells appears in the Time Machine.

Wells: Hello! Don't tell me – you've got problems.

Mudd: Disaster!

Samantha: Chaos!

Groove: We'd have been better off the way we were.

Wells: Well look, I did warn you. I mean choosing the change that's best for you is only half the battle. A good manager also learns the skills needed to implement those changes. And there are three simple steps which are: **Analyse the gap. Plan the route. Manage the journey**.

Groove: Sounds like what we were trying to do.

Wells: Yes, well . . . perhaps I'd better find out just what you've been up to.

Groove: Well, for a start, look what happened to me last Tuesday . . .

Wells: Last Tuesday? Right, let's see . . .

Once again, the familiar buttons are pressed. The scene shows a besieged Groove at his desk, which is awash with paperwork. He is on the phone, signing a sheaf of documents which his secretary waits to take away, as Geoff Bull, Transport Manager, enters in an aggressive mood.

Groove: Look, all I can say is, tell them that when the warehouse . . . Hang on a minute . . . Geoff, you're a bit early.

Geoff: This won't take long.

Groove: I'm sorry, I'll have to hang up. I've got the Transport Manager here. As I . . . just tell them that when the warehousing is centralised, the managers will be able to make their orders as they always have done. Oh, well look, just keep them happy. Goodbye.

Geoff: You do realise that my drivers are up in arms about all this.

Groove: About all this?

Geoff: About this move to Shifnal. I don't know if I can keep the lid on this any longer . . .

Groove: Well, hold on . . . Shifnal?

Geoff: Outside of Wolverhampton. Back of beyond . . .

Groove: Yes, I know where it is . . . what about it?

Geoff: The new central warehouse. Of course, nobody told me about it, but apparently the drivers have heard that's where it's going to be.

Groove: And where did they get that from?

Geoff: That's where Slikstore have relocated, and they've had big problems.

Groove: Buyworld are not Slikstore.

Geoff: Had to get rid of drivers . . .

Groove: Look, Geoff, you know damn well this is a complex operation. And when it's all over, everybody'll see that the changes aren't as bad as they imagined.

Geoff: So we'll be keeping up our force of drivers?

Groove: Yes, yes – twenty-five, twenty-six. Look, I haven't worked out every little detail . . .

Geoff: That's not a little detail. If you're driver twenty-six, that's your job gone.

Groove: Yes, well they shouldn't listen to rumours.

Geoff: But that's all they're hearing. Look, the drivers are having a meeting this afternoon, and I have to tell you there's talk of a ban on overtime.

Groove: Oh, for Christ's sake!

Geoff: Can I tell the drivers categorically we are not going to Shifnal, and there will be no redundancies?

Groove: Yes, yes. Tell them anything you like.

Geoff: They won't believe it. And neither do I.

The scene fades and Groove looks accusingly at Wells.

Groove: Well, what am I supposed to say when they start jumping to conclusions, demanding answers?

Wells: Well, there are some questions to which the correct answer is 'I don't know'.

Groove: Oh, very impressive – oh yes, that is good management.

Wells: Yes, yes it is, because good management means working together to find the answer – what's the point of bluffing? Reassuring people that things aren't going to change?

Groove: Well . . . obviously we've told people things are going to be different.

Wells: Yes, but you haven't actually worked out *how* different. And that is Step One in implementing change. You have to: **Analyse the gap**. List the main differences between where you are now, and where you intend to be.

Groove: You mean actually list all the differences for each department, each procedure, every single person? I can't do all that!

Wells: No, not on your own you can't, so use your staff to help you get the complete picture. Involve everyone in a positive approach to the change.

Groove: Well, it makes sense in theory, I suppose. All right, all right. I'll try it with Geoff tomorrow.

Wells: Good. Let's see how you get on.

More buttons – and the scene is tomorrow.

Geoff: I don't believe this! You've called me in here to tell me you don't know?

Groove: That's right. Until we've got a clearer picture of what these changes are going to involve, well I daren't honestly tell you how many driving hours we're going to need.

Geoff: Look, I know the whole reason behind this was to expand the business. But that doesn't necessarily mean more drivers, does it?

Groove: We aim to be serving more outlets. On the other hand, long-haul bulk deliveries mean fewer runs.

Geoff: And that might require two-man teams in the cab.

Groove: Well, here's the sort of schedule that

Marketing envisage. Can you and your drivers let me know what handling that will involve from your point of view?

Geoff: Well, this is going to cut down the number of runs on some routes – but we'd need to work out a new leave rota, which would complicate the picture.

Groove: Exactly how is the new operation going to affect your drivers?

Geoff: Well, I don't know. But I can find out.

Watching, Mudd is impressed . . .

Mudd: Well, that looks a bit more promising.

Wells: Just remember Step One. Analyse the gap and list the main differences betwen where you are now, and where you intend to be.

Groove: Very helpful, thank you.

Wells: Not at all.

Samantha: Not so fast. I did all that, and I'm no better off than Mr Groove was.

Wells: Ah now, if I remember, you convinced your colleagues at Actiontogs to move into the field of leisurewear for the older customer, based on the increasing proportion of that age group in the population.

Samantha: Yes, and we analysed the gap very thoroughly.

Wells: So all of you knew exactly what you were aiming for?

Samantha: I thought we did – but the department is running around in all directions like a . . . a bunch of headless chickens.

Wells: Can you give me an example?

Samantha: Any time, any day, in the last three months!

Wells: Oh well, let's have a look then.

Wells shuts his eyes and presses buttons at random. Samantha is in her office and Janet rushes in . . .

Janet: I've had Quality Control on the phone.
Samantha: Well, you sort it out, Janet.
Janet: The fabrics have shrunk in the test wash, the batch colours are different and the reds and blues aren't fast.
Samantha: Chase them up again.
Janet: I already did, this morning. They might get bolshie if I keep chasing them.
Samantha: Well, make them bolshie. We can't give the go-ahead to manufacture until we've solved these problems. Ah Julian . . .

Julian, Manager of the local Actiontogs branch, bursts in with a bale of over-sixties leisurewear. He is in a state and dumps the clothes on Samantha's desk.

Julian: Talk about shoddy workmanship! Just look, . . . look at those zips. What cowboy outfit threw these samples together? The Wild Bunch?
Samantha: Janet, get me Jerkin and Breeks.
Julian: Jerkin and Breeks? No wonder it's rubbish. I told you we should have stuck with Cladrags. They did wonders for our toddler wear last year.
Samantha: Yes, Cladrags are very good, but they couldn't produce the garments in time.
Julian: You mean *you* didn't give them the time.
Samantha: Whereas Jerkin and Breeks *could* get the clothes to meet the deadline.
Julian: Well, it's a pity they couldn't get them to meet in the middle.

The scene fades and a miserable Samantha is close to tears.

> **Samantha:** I can't bear to watch. I mean, everybody knew exactly where we were aiming for . . .
> **Wells:** Come on, into the Machine with you.
> **Samantha:** Where are we going?
> **Wells:** Back to square one. Three months ago, before all those problems started happening. Let's see if you can make sure they never do.

They vanish, and the scene moves back three months to Samantha's office where she is in a meeting with Janet and Julian.

> **Samantha:** OK, we all know what we're out to achieve, and we mustn't lose heart just because we can foresee problems.
> **Julian:** The main one being that Cladrags can't handle the order. Not on the proposed time-scale.

Abruptly Wells snaps her back to the present.

> **Wells:** But they didn't know how to get there, you see. Without sensible planning, their journey turned into some crazy kind of initiative test, instead of being a properly planned expedition. And that is Step Two. You must: **Plan the route**. Decide on steps to help you all progress from your present state to your future state. Examine what could help and hinder on the way.
> **Samantha:** You mean, if we hadn't tried to rush headlong through the whole thing, we wouldn't have come up against all those unexpected hazards?
> **Wells:** Right. With a properly planned route, you can avoid all the detours and black spots and bottlenecks.

Samantha: So the whole team need to work out that route together.

Wells: Tell you what – hop on, have another go.

And off they go.

Samantha: OK, we all know what we're out to achieve, and we mustn't lose heart just because we can foresee problems.

Julian: The main one being that Cladrags can't handle the order. Not on the proposed time-scale.

Janet: Jerkin and Breeks say they can do it.

Julian: Yes, but look at the standard of their work. And the older customers are very particular about a garment's quality and finish.

Janet: Look, I know you want to get this over with as soon as possible, but aren't we making this changeover too fast to be practical?

Samantha: But we can't do it gradually. We've got to have a launch date, make a splash, bang the drum . . .

Julian: Well, look, what about my idea of a staggered launch? Area by area. Bang a whole succession of drums.

Janet: It would take the pressure off.

Samantha: And it could increase our coverage.

Janet: It could even give us the sort of delivery schedule Cladrags could meet.

Julian: Then we'd be sure of getting quality garments.

Samantha: Now we're getting somewhere . . .

For the moment that somewhere is back, or rather forward, with Mudd and Groove.

Groove: Welcome back. Got everything sorted out, all your problems?

Samantha: What problems?

Mudd: I thought you were having problems.

Samantha: Who, us? No, no, everything's fine, always has been. Right from the start I consulted our people and got them to contribute positive ideas, raise any practical problems, and generally make clear everyone's understanding of the task ahead.

Groove: In other words, Step Two.

Samantha: Exactly. All you have to do is – Plan the route. Decide on steps to help you all progress from your present state to your future state. Examine what could help and hinder on the way.

Mudd: So now you have no problems?

Samantha: None.

Mudd: Well all I can say is you've been damn lucky. We've ended up with as many problems as we started with. Our change was to go over to a flexitime working system – you know, plastic clocking-in cards to register the staff's cumulative hours.

Wells: Sounds sensible enough.

Mudd: A great idea, but when I fired the starting gun, everything went bananas. Productivity, morale, right up the spout. And everything came to a head a month ago.

Wells: I suppose we'd better look into this.

The scene shows Louise, one of the clerks, sitting by the desk, sniffing and clearly upset. Mudd, very ill at ease, paces about.

Mudd: Louise, look . . . I . . . well look, the fact remains that your work just isn't up to scratch.

Louise: What's that supposed to mean?

Mudd: This backlog. Look, there are people here who've been waiting seven weeks for a licence. Some of them have applied more than once . . .

Louise: All right . . .

Mudd: No, it's not all right, is it?

Louise: Those are all cases with queries against them.

Mudd: But you and Brenda used to be able to keep up to date with them.

Louise: When we had a chance to discuss things. But she's got to go and pick up the kids at four. And Brenda never stops for lunch now, so she's always in a foul mood.

Mudd: But the reason we introduced flexitime was to make things easier for everyone.

Louise: The work isn't easier.

Mudd: So . . . what about the hours you've been putting in. This past four weeks. It's in the file. Just 30 hours, 31 hours, 28 hours . . .

Louise: That's up to me, isn't it? And I'm always here for the core time, 11 till 3. That's all I'm obliged to do.

Mudd: But you're not getting the work done, are you?

Louise: Why are you picking on me?

Mudd: I'm not. I'll tell Brenda and Kevin the same thing. Until we clear this backlog, I want you and the others at your desks from 9 o'clock until 5.30. Let's have a little discipline for a change.

Louise: Have you got a dictionary?

Mudd: What for?

Louise: I want to look up the meaning of 'flexitime'.

As time moves on Mudd naturally wants an explanation from Wells.

Mudd: So what happened? I just can't understand it.

The staff were all so co-operative and enthusiastic when we were planning the change to flexitime, but when we put it into practice . . . well, they really let me down.

Wells: Did they?

Mudd: Are you suggesting it was my fault?

Wells: May I introduce you to Step Three, which is: **Manage the journey**. Provide resources to take the steps. Support and train those involved.

Mudd: I'm sorry, I'm all at sea.

Wells: So are your staff, and that's the problem. Look, change means re-learning; and that can be painful, because it means un-learning first.

Mudd: Well, at least with the old timetable everyone knew where they were, or where they were supposed to be.

Wells: Precisely. That was their anchor. Now it's been taken away – it's no wonder they're feeling apprehensive and vulnerable.

Mudd: And obstructive and inefficient?

Wells: Look, going over to flexitime has meant you've all been confronted with the completely new responsibility of how to manage your own time.

Mudd: Of course! They haven't learned how to cope; that's why they're letting me down. Or perhaps it's why *I'm* letting them down. But what should I do?

Wells: Oh, you'll think of something. In fact, I'm going to watch you do it next week . . .

The screen comes to life, showing Mudd addressing the staff.

Mudd: Now, as you all know, I was the first of several managers to recommend to the Executive Committee that we went over to a system of flexible working hours. After due consideration, they decided to implement our suggestion. Naturally I . . . and you . . . played our part in working out exactly what the changeover would mean, and indeed we all planned the operation very carefully, and since then have been working with the new system. Some of you might say working in spite of the new system? Because, let's be honest, it has caused us some problems. Yes, Louise?

Louise: Does this mean we'll be going back to the old timetable?

Mudd: Certainly not.

Louise: Thank goodness. We all still agree that flexitime ought to be the answer. We just didn't expect the adjustment to be so difficult.

Mudd: No we didn't. And I didn't understand why until . . . well, anyway . . . yesterday I consulted the Executive Committee and it turns out we're not the only ones with problems. So, following my suggestion, they are going to circulate some leaflets on time management. They may even set up a short lecture course, because that's at the root of the trouble. We all have to learn the most effective way to organise our own time. Now we're finding it a bit strange but please, if any of you have any queries or find any problems developing, come and see me. Between us we'll find the answers, or get the right advice. OK? Any questions?

All hands immediately go up in the air.

Mudd: I was afraid of that . . .

And so it is over to the time traveller for the last time.

Wells: Well, never mind – it's a start. The right start

and you'll never get to your destination if you don't take the trouble to begin.

Mudd: Got it. So that's the third step in implementing change.

Wells: Can we have a re-cap?

Groove: Step One. Analyse the gap. List the main differences between where you are now, and where you want to be. In my case that meant involving everybody in working out what effect the proposed changes would have on them and their jobs.

Samamtha: Step Two. Plan the route. Decide on steps to help you *all* progress from your present state to your future state. Examine what could help and hinder on the way. In my case that meant not rushing to get the change over and done with as soon as possible, but planning it carefully, one stage at a time.

Mudd: And Step Three. Manage the journey. Provide the resources to take the steps. Support and train those involved. In my case that meant not leaving everyone to adapt to the unfamiliar ncw system as best they could, but providing information and advice to help us all learn how to cope with change.

Wells: Good. So now you all know how to choose and implement the changes that are best for you. But, remember this one thing about the future – you never get there. So keep looking and planning ahead. And now, I really must fly, so if you'll forgive me . . .

Groove: Mr Wells, we're all very grateful for your advice. I wonder, before you go, would you be kind enough to autograph this book?

Wells: Oh certainly, yes. What's it called?

Groove: *The War of the Worlds.*

Samantha: It's a classic – been a bestseller for a hundred years.

Wells: Really? Who wrote it?

Mudd: You did!

Wells: Did I? What year?

Groove: 1898.

Wells: Ah! . . . look, I'm on my way back to 1895. Do you think I could take this with me, only it would save rather a lot of work . . . Thanks so much.

Wells and the Time Machine vanish . . .

Golden rules

1 Explain your changes to those affected.
2 Don't be afraid to admit what you don't know and can't predict.
3 Change is a journey and needs planning step by step.
4 All changes have consequences; make sure you anticipate the likely ones.
5 Change needs to be 'sold'; there is always resistance and reasons and advantages have to be spelled out.